MORE THAN
GRASSHOPPERS

LEE ANN ALEXANDER
JOEL ALEXANDER

MORE THAN GRASSHOPPERS

RECLAIMING YOUR GOD-GIVEN IDENTITY

WORD AFLAME PRESS
8855 Dunn Road, Hazelwood, MO 63042
www.pentecostalpublishing.com

All Scripture quotations in this book are from the New King James Version of the Bible unless otherwise identified.

Scripture verses marked (NKJV) from the New King James Version, copyright © 1982 by Thomas Nelson, Inc.; verses marked (NLT) from the New Living Translation®, copyright © 1996, 2004, 2007, Tyndale House Publishers, Inc., Carol Stream, Illinois 60188.

Cover design by Timothy Burk

Library of Congress Cataloging-in-Publication Data

Names: Alexander, Lee Ann, 1979- author.
Title: More than grasshoppers : reclaiming your God-given identity / by Lee Ann and Joel Alexander.
Description: Hazelwood : Word Aflame Press, 2016.
Identifiers: LCCN 2016023751 | ISBN 9780757752148 (alk. paper)
Subjects: LCSH: Identity (Psychology)--Religious aspects--Christianity. | Pentecostal churches--Doctrines.
Classification: LCC BV4509.5 .A44 2016 | DDC 248.4--dc23 LC record available at https://lccn.loc.gov/2016023751

For our parents,
Mark and Judy Alexander,
who have a reckless belief in us and yet by example cultivated in us
an absolute dependence on God.

And now to the Abbyss I pass
Of that unfathomable Grass,
Where Men like Grashoppers appear,
But Grashoppers are Gyants there:
They, in there squeking Laugh, contemn
Us as we walk more low then them:
And, from the Precipices tall
Of the green spir's, to us do call.
　　—xlvii

　　"Upon Appleton House"
　　by Andrew Marvell (1681)

CONTENTS

PREFACE

You're about to journey into a secret place: the terrain of your own heart. Over the course of twenty chapters, you will be challenged to analyze your own identity.

We encourage you to enjoy the journey. The authors have included stories throughout the book to make the expedition enjoyable, and they've intentionally used a casual writing style to create a conversation with you. For the sake of uniformity, Lee Ann has written the stories from her point of view unless otherwise indicated. However, the premise of the book originated with Joel's study, and his insight gave it shape.

For your personal study, follow the prayer prompt at the conclusion of each chapter so the Lord may mold and transform the way you think and feel about yourself.

Questions for reflection are also included at the end of each chapter. You may use the questions for self-evaluation. Additionally, the book can be used for a group study in a book club, church small group, or any number of formats. In any one of those scenarios the questions for reflection can be used to facilitate group discussion. We pray that the Spirit will guide your conversation as the body of Christ ministers one to another during your group study.

Whatever the format, we pray that as you open your mind and heart to the voice of God, He will call you to your rightful place in His kingdom as His heir.

ACKNOWLEDGMENTS

A wise man once said there is nothing new under the sun. While this book is the result of prayer, study, and the authors' deliberation of Pentecostal anthropology, the contents are also a result of the influence of a host of great men and women of God. Lee Ann thanks the faculty and staff of Gateway College of Evangelism, Urshan College, and Urshan Graduate School of Theology for profoundly shaping her worldview and theology. Joel wishes to thank his fellow laborers in the Florida district of the United Pentecostal Church International and the personal influence of Bishop C. P. Williams. He also honors his wife, Jessica, for her love and support.

Both authors pay tribute to their home church in Denham Springs, Louisiana, for a firm foundation. They honor Rev. and Mrs. W. R. Johnson for lifelong impact. They also thank Rev. and Mrs. Richie Driver, Rev. and Mrs. Tony Roberts, Rev. and Mrs. Billy Johnson, and an army of Sunday school teachers and youth volunteers whose labor and influence guided the authors through a range of seasons leading to lives dedicated to ministry.

Finally, this book is a result of the ministry of Pentecostal Publishing House. The authors are grateful for the thoughtful work of Everett Gossard and Robin Johnston, who edit with precision and a vision for the most effective way to impart scriptural principles. The authors also are thankful for the design, production, and management expertise of Tim Cummings, Mark Blackburn, Jim Sample, Abraham LaVoi, Larry Craig, and the rest of the wonderful PPH team committed to the vital work of resourcing the church.

CHAPTER 1

INTRODUCTION

Consider the scene: God had given His people an incredible promise of victory and abundance. A select group of men, whom we should assume represented respected leaders among the people since they were entrusted with such a task, embarked on a scouting expedition. They encountered the enemy, the potential conquest, and their own fears. They did the math, and their true self-image affected the sum total: "We are but grasshoppers." And with that, ten men sealed the fate of their generation as wanderers who could not receive God's promise of triumph and abundance.

Those flunky undercover agents from the Old Testament don't have a corner on the market when it comes to messed-up self-worth, identity, and destiny. While our culture bogs further and further in revolting narcissism, Joshuas, Gideons, and Samsons falter in our churches—each is a symbol for identity struggles. We have too many Gideons in hiding who cannot see themselves as the mighty man of valor God can see underneath the fear and insecurities. We need some Joshuas who fight off the inferiority complex that our doubt-riddled flesh and the enemy himself would try to impose. And we need some redeemed Samsons of ability who throw off the temptation of arrogance and dedicate their talents to God in humility.

As we began writing this book, after Joel presented a portion in a student workers' training seminar, we frequently confronted the reality that we are not professional therapists. Yet in serving in a combination of roles as student pastor, student advisor in a college setting, and in a number of informal counseling sessions as ministers, we have seen countless people of all ages struggling to understand their identity and worth. In fact, as we consulted with various ministers and editors on the creation of this book and explained the thesis, a couple of consultants asked, "Oh, so this is a book for youth?" I wish it were only adolescents who battled with their worth. I wish men in their mid-forties and women in their fifties and preteens being bullied and senior adults in nursing homes never faced identity assaults. I wish cultivating a God-centered self-image was something we worked through as sixteen- and seventeen-year-olds and then graduated to live secure, stable Apostolic lives never to be rattled by identity questions. Yet the statistics and the struggles of people we encounter weekly reflect an epidemic of identity issues that rock Christians of all ages.

Iconic Pentecostal leader T. F. Tenney claims, "We are living in a world in an identity crisis. People simply do not know who they are, or who they are supposed to be. The society in which we operate is in trouble. . . . As Apostolics, we must find our true identity, knowing it is when we find God's destiny for our lives, then and only then will we know—and become—who we are meant to be."[1]

Let's get personal. Who are you? Before you read any further, describe yourself in three words—the first words that pop in your head.

What did you come up with? Did you go with the words that came to mind first or did you dismiss them and find others? Why?

If you were the rebel who read straight through the activity without playing along (what does that say about you?), we are going to give you a second chance to be a team player. Take the next ten seconds to close your eyes and think of three things you like about yourself. Close your eyes and go.

Okay, before you analyze those qualities, we are going to do yet another activity. You'll have another ten seconds. This time, you'll think of three things you don't like about yourself. Go.

Okay, take a deep breath. Besides reflecting on the self-image diagnosis involved in the words you chose, ask yourself this question: which was easier—identifying qualities you liked about yourself or those you don't?

I've conducted this exercise several times in classes and the overwhelming majority of people can find an infinite list of things they don't like about themselves—faults, flaws, and shortcomings of all stripes from their uneven earlobes to destructive addictions—while most people struggle to come up with even a few positive qualities about themselves.

In this book we're going to argue that Apostolic Christians are plagued with self-image problems resulting from an identity crisis. Because we don't understand how God thinks about us, we don't know how to think about ourselves. I'm not peddling a "power of positive thinking" knock-off; I'm talking about looking to Scripture to realign the most foundational aspects of our thinking: who God is, what He thinks of us, and then how we should think of ourselves.

Who do you think you are? I intentionally want to push you on that point. You must understand yourself, and to do that, you first must understand who God thinks you are.

We so often see ourselves as inferior: just grasshoppers. Do we have any sense of how God sees us? Do we really get that He loves us? Do we honor the privilege of being made in His image? Do we let the hunger for acceptance by and affirmation of others shape our sense of worth and manipulate our behaviors? Do we struggle with feelings of low self-confidence or ricochet to the extreme of arrogance over our perceived strengths and talents?

Failure to see who we are in Christ is failure to understand the grace and power of God. It's a blindness to all of the many verses in the Bible that declare the limitless power of Jesus Christ. He can do anything, even—in fact, especially—through you.

Seeing ourselves as less than what we are is a trick of the enemy. And the sad part is, it's contagious. The grasshopper effect represents the tendency to see ourselves as less than we really are in God, exaggerate who the enemy is, and spread that poison to others.

The Bible is filled with grasshoppers—men and women who thought themselves inadequate, unqualified, or somehow falling short when stacked alongside perceived competition. And yet it is as if God seems to particularly delight in using just such people to experience the miraculous and in turn change the world around them. The issue is entirely in our self-perception—our willingness to accept our identity as Jesus-name, Holy-Ghost-empowered Apostolics. This book is a challenge to change the way you see yourself—to understand your rightful place as a child of God made in His image, bearing His name, and filled with His Spirit.

CHAPTER 2

THE ANATOMY OF GRASSHOPPERS

They'd just crossed the Red Sea—that like-nothing-you've-ever-heard-about miraculous event that even Hollywood can't resist trying to portray with every new advancement in film technology. You would think a miracle like that would've sucked away any lingering doubts about the power of this Yahweh. Then there had been those terrifying moments after they complained and God sent fatal fire, as well as another round of sheer, magnificent terror after Miriam and Aaron questioned Moses and God smacked them down. In retrospect, they probably figured out that doubting was stupid. But it happens when Yahweh doesn't deliver on the promise the way you expect.

Even though God had long since promised the land of their dreams was theirs, it's a funny thing about faith. You don't have to choose to doubt. It just happens—the default position. You have to choose not to.

Still, when God instructed Moses to commission a scouting expedition, He reminded him it was "the land of Canaan, which I am giving to [you]" (Numbers 13:2). And so Moses gave the charge to check out this promised land and its people. You can't help but wonder if these undercover operatives heard in Moses' directions the possibility of failure. Why did Moses care if the Canaanites were strong or weak, few or many (Numbers 13:18)? Why would it matter since God had promised to give them the land? But for whatever reason, God had directed Moses to send scouts, so a full report was in order. And with that charge, the tribal leaders packed their knapsacks, donned their camouflage, and started their mission.

For forty days they infiltrated the land—likely the area between the Mediterranean Sea and the Jordan River. And the land lived up to the hype. We still sing songs about the "milk and honey flowing" and every Sunday school teacher worth her salt has wowed kids with the story of grapes so big it took two men to carry them.

But the people in the land—there's the rub. Most of our problems don't involve resources of money, land, buildings, or technology; most of our problems are people problems. It was no different for the Israelites, and their people problems were giants. Scholars have done work to track down the details about these giants. Yet in the context of God's promise, does it really matter if they were seven feet tall or nine feet tall or nineteen feet tall? Whatever their statistics, when the operatives returned home, the die had been cast. You know the report: the land is incredible! But the cities are . . . huge and hard to attack. And the people? Well . . . they are fierce and they are huge (Numbers 13:27–28).

I guess we'll never know exactly what was going through Caleb's mind, but he interrupted the lead CIA agent. With no rebuttal or point of information to correct the aforementioned details, he cut to the chase and threw down the challenge: "'Let us go up at once and take possession, for we are well able to overcome it'" (Numbers 13:30).

At this point you have to wonder if his comrades felt betrayed. I can imagine that one guy on the team across the circle giving him the "shut-up" stink eye while another close by hissed, "What are you doing?!" On one level, I almost get it; they were scared. Their report was not untruthful, just one-sided.

And so they bounded back, "'We are not able to go up against the people, for they are stronger than we'" (Numbers 13:31). Worse than just debating hypothetical battle outcomes, they went among the people spreading their scary news and pessimism. In their propaganda, they wedged a telling diagnosis: "'There we saw the giants (the descendants of Anak came from the giants); and we were like grasshoppers in our own sight, and so we were in their sight.'"

Not only did the spies feel they were miniscule, they projected that their enemies shared the estimation. You can study the Hebrew variation for the word *grasshopper* and the use of animal metaphors in Scripture, but all signs point to the idea that the spies were emphasizing how small and helpless they felt in comparison to their enemy. The irony is that when a group of these same insects worked together, they could destroy a people's food source and consequently defeat an entire society. Yet the spies only focused on their own insecurities. Given the agrarian nature of biblical culture, a united swarm of grasshoppers was your worst nightmare. In II Chronicles 7:13, God spoke of using similar insects to ravage the land, and Joel compared a grasshopper swarm to a conquering army (Joel 2:25). In fact, the spies characterized themselves as puny grasshoppers or locusts after having just seen God use such creatures to plague Egypt in a history-changing way. Old Testament scholar Berl Dov Lerner argues, "The spies imagined their enemies regarding them as helpless grasshoppers. . . . Their

7

enemies did indeed view them as grasshoppers, not tiny individual grasshoppers, but rather an enormous unstoppable horde of grasshoppers, a locust swarm which would destroy all in its path."[1] It's a matter of perspective, and for the Israelites, perspective was a problem.

Professor Robert Morosco has conducted thorough theological study of Numbers 13 and takes the issue of perspective a step further. He theorizes that what you fear ultimately reveals your faith:

> From a purely psychological perspective, it seems almost unfair that God should so react to the fear of man. After all, were not the circumstances such that anyone with any sense would have been afraid to enter the territory of the powerful Canaanites? This kind of thinking, though dominated with concern, fails to fully grasp the theological implications of fear. . . . The people esteemed man over God, and so usurped God's throne. . . . The spies and the people were trusting in the ability of the Canaanites over and above that of the living God, and this was their tragic sin (Matthew 10:28). . . . When the Exodus generation exhibited their fear of the Canaanites by accepting their will over Jehovah's, they, in essence, had elevated the power and impendency of the Canaanites over the omnipotence and imminence of God, who was with Israel.[2]

Morosco's insight is challenging, but he misses something else: their sin was not just in their failure to see God's ability but also their failure to see the abilities He had put in them. Could it be that God was frustrated that they had no vision for the conquering army God had made them to be? This tension reveals something potent about our identity: who we are is determined by who we think we are, and all of that is wrapped up in our understanding of who God is and who He has created us to be.

Sounds rather convoluted, right? Rewind back to tenth-grade geometry class and all of those complex word problems. Mathematicians devised a system to break down such quandaries using a series of theorems to come up with a proof. Applied to the topic of our God-given identity, let's illustrate it as such:

Given: God made us. Prove: God wants us to have a healthy identity rooted in Him.	
Statement	**Reason**
1. God makes good things.	Mark 7:37
2. God handcrafted us in His image.	Genesis 1:27
3. God loves us and sees value in us.	John 3:16
4. When we are baptized in His name and filled with His Spirit, we are restored to intimate relationship with Him and become led of His Spirit.	Romans 5; Romans 8:14
5. God empowers us with both personal talents and spiritual gifts.	Romans 8:37
6. Because God made us in His image, loves us, and empowers us for victorious living, we should feel complete in our identity in Him.	

This book will build the case that once we understand our true identity in Jesus Christ, we should reflect that identity in the way we treat others and serve in advancing God's kingdom.

CHAPTER 3

GRASSHOPPERS INDEED

I n 1957 Random House published *Atlas Shrugged* by Ayn Rand, a Russian philosopher reacting to the fallout of socialist politics. Besides being hefty enough to anchor a sizable boat, the novel presented a scenario where society collapsed because its most talented and brilliant workers resigned from their professions and abandoned society. At the risk of doing a deep injustice to Rand, I'll give you a cheat-sheet version of her philosophy known as egotism: the individual reigns supreme; the most-talented, smartest, and hardest-working "producers" create and sustain society; and self is the highest power.

Rand's mid-twentieth-century exaltation of human abilities was not unique to a certain time period. Typically the way we assess human nature goes to one extreme or another: we either think we are invincible or incompetent. And since history bears record of good men and women achieving many remarkable things, it's easy to see the individual as unstoppable.

The truth of the matter is, we are not invincible. We do have limitations. We want to believe in people—in the goodness of humanity and all the potentials and possibilities of the individual. We want the good guy to win and we want a hero in a white hat to prevail. Think about it; Disney has created an empire from one formula repeated over and over and over: an ordinary person (maybe even a mouse) gets into trouble but digs deep to battle his or her way through adversity and wins in the end. But Disney does not author our lives' stories.

Let's go back to the twelve spies. They described themselves as grasshoppers. Were they? Maybe there was a bit of hyperbole in their report, but compared to the giants, they were somewhat smaller. If God is going to get angry every time we exaggerate, no one should ever go fishing again and our family reunions just got a lot less entertaining. Yet apparently there is a danger in hyperbole and being flexible with absolute truth.

God did care that the Israelites called themselves grasshoppers. The truth is that truth is a big deal to God. Telling untruths made the big Ten (Exodus 20:16). Scripture goes on to say lying is an abomination (Proverbs 12:22) and that God hates it (Proverbs 6:16–17). We have Sunday school lessons about not telling white lies because we recognize the importance of teaching the smallest of children the danger of accepting even the slightest degree of unrighteousness. We simply must commit to absolute truth because deception is the enemy of allowing God sovereign reign. Whether we are deceiving others or we are deceiving ourselves, deception blocks the forthright working of the Spirit in our lives. God cannot be Master of everything if we create alternate realities that color the truth. God is perfect, and while we are human, we are to pursue truthfulness and accuracy: "A just weight is his delight" (Proverbs 11:1); "But he who does the truth comes to the light, that his deeds may be clearly seen, that they have been done in God" (John 3:21); "speaking the truth in love, may grow up in all things into Him who is the head—Christ" (Ephesians 4:15). Deception is a heart problem and a vision problem. Is it any stretch then to say that God gets frustrated when we lie to ourselves about ourselves—in either direction of inflated or undercut self-worth? So when the spies spun the report, God got angry.

Their grasshopper statement also indicates a vision problem. They thought little of themselves not necessarily because they were sitting around wanting to lie but because they could not or chose not to see themselves for who they were.

Truthfully, if you considered the statistics, the Israelites were outsized and outnumbered, and the giants had the home field advantage. All things considered, they were grasshoppers indeed. The difference kicks in when we look to God, and that makes all the difference.

At least two alternate versions of the spy story could have happened instead. Option #1: God could have wiped out the enemy without the children of Israel having to fight at all. This version of history would have sped through a barrel-load of whining and tantrums and whether through a plague or a poof, God's promise would have been accomplished. Option #2: God could have vanquished the giants and left medium-sized warriors the Israelites could have squared off against on their own. Yet God chose to leave these giants standing between His people and His promise.

Over and over in Scripture a pattern emerges of grasshoppers against giants. Godless people speak of David and Goliath to indicate seemingly uneven odds, all a result of an unqualified young Israelite facing an impossibility. Why are God's people always up against such towering walls and extra-menacing opponents? Could it be that God wants us to fully depend on Him and give Him all the glory? When facing a particularly nasty thorn in the flesh, Paul's word from God was, "My strength is made perfect in weakness" (II Corinthians 12:9).

I refuse to let it go without saying: we need Jesus. The thesis of this book is that we should be secure in the knowledge that God made us to be more than conquerors, but that is only because of God working through us. There is a difference between having a healthy identity and being self-sufficient. The former understands we are good because we are God's; the latter overlooks the need for God. The minute we rest in our own abilities without turning to God, we negate those abilities that are in fact given by God. We ought to be thankful for our limitations if they drive us to a rightful place of dependency on Jesus Christ.

The truth is . . . we are grasshoppers.

*　*　*　*　*

Though the focus of this book is the Numbers 13 grasshopper story, grasshoppers pop up other places in the Bible.

> Have you not known? Have you not heard? Has it not been told you from the beginning? Have you not understood from the foundations of the earth? It is He who sits above the circle of the earth, And its inhabitants are like grasshoppers (Isaiah 40:21–22).

Hold everything. Did God just call us grasshoppers? Is He saying we are puny? First of all, it is not uncommon to run across an animal metaphor in Scripture given the agrarian culture, much like we would say, "I've got the Monday blues," showing that the standard North American calendar dictates our lives. However, just as the sentiment of our emotions being controlled by a calendar is problematic, the spies' lack of trust in God and who He made them to be was a problem, whatever the metaphor used.

No, the message of Isaiah 40 is that God is sovereign, and we would do well to remember that we serve Him and not the other way around. Isaiah later records, "'For My thoughts are not your thoughts, Nor are your ways My ways,' says the Lord. 'For as the heavens are higher than the earth, So are My ways higher than your ways, And My thoughts than your thoughts" (Isaiah 55:8–9). We are grasshoppers compared to God, plain and simple. But we are not grasshoppers compared to the problems of life because that big and mighty God who made every grasshopper is with us. That foundation gives us all the hope we need to face anything life or the enemy throws our way.

Do we have our flaws? Do we have grasshopper weaknesses? Sure, but it doesn't matter when we know who our God is. God can use us not just in spite of our weaknesses but because of them. They turn us toward Him and help us rely on Him and not ourselves.

Psychologists released a study recently that claimed college-aged people are more self-centered than generations past. One author dug into that phenomenon and summarized the findings:

> We've gone overboard in telling our children how special they are, when we should be showing them their responsibilities to others. The study suggests that narcissists "are more likely to have romantic relationships that are short-lived, at risk for infidelity, lack of emotional warmth, and to exhibit game-playing, dishonesty, and over-controlling and violent behaviors." Also, those with high scores on the inventory are more likely to cheat on tests. The researchers believe that the

self-esteem movement, beginning in the 1980s,
has something to do with this trend.[1]

It saddens me that in trying to fix an identity problem, we've only perpetuated the problem. Well-meaning but misguided parents who recognized an ailment treated it with wrong medicine. If only we could get through to parents, educators, and people of every walk of life: the answer for coping with identity problems and lack of self-worth is not to sponsor an ego-feeding frenzy! Our hope for a settled identity is to help every person understand who they are because of who God has made us to be and His work in our lives.

The spies got it wrong. It wasn't that the grasshopper label was that far off; it was their failure to recognize they needed to turn to God and see the situation as an opportunity for God to do the miraculous.

We have to believe that God can and will use us. Simple, right? Unfortunately many people can't get their minds around that for a variety of reasons. Let's handle one thing right now: you are not worthy of God's love. There's probably a more Dale Carnegie-ish way of saying that, but I'll cut to the chase: there is nothing any one of us has done of ourselves that is worth God's love and what happened on Calvary. But because He loves us and went to Calvary of His own volition, the blood He shed there makes us worthy. To go a step further, because of that blood, we are also made holy to serve His kingdom.

Unfortunately many people have a fundamental lack of faith regarding this principle of being used by God. Think of how few people are used in the gifts of the Spirit. Is God not able to work through people? Is God not wanting to work through people? Or could it be that we are lacking faith to be used in the gifts because of our own issues we can't get past?

We must acknowledge that God wants to use us. If we rewind to the book's opening exercise where we listed all of our negative qualities, we quickly see our tendency to recite a list of reasons why God cannot use us. To do so is to insult God's power to work through us.

Developing an active faith in God is a prerequisite to having an Apostolic identity. And developing such a faith requires a frequent diet of reflection on the power of God and the countless examples from the Bible of people God used despite significant shortcomings.

Let me put it this way. Yes, we need to recognize our limitations. But rather than letting those limitations and weaknesses lock us into a perpetual cycle of rejecting God's redeeming and empowering transformative work that equips us to serve in His kingdom, those limitations should propel us to immerse ourselves in God's presence and commit to serving this great God who so mercifully redeemed and empowered us.

In the Sermon on the Mount, Jesus identified several qualities that result in blessing (Matthew 5:1–11). However, if you look at the list (mourning, being poor in spirit, meekness, being persecuted, and showing mercy), those traits don't typically describe our world's lists of powerful and successful people. That seemingly incongruous tension simply reflects that the yielding of our human nature to make room for Jesus to work in our lives is the key to opening our lives for God to move. Author Kyle Idleman explains:

> Jesus is describing people who know they don't have it all figured out, people who are humble enough to ask for help. This world's success puts the emphasis on being self-sufficient and self-reliant, acting as if we've got it all figured out. But Jesus redefines a successful life as one that

humbly says to God, "I can't do this on my own.
I need your help." From the world's perspective,
that's the opposite of what successful people do.[2]

The Christian practice of self-effacement is unheard of in today's world or misunderstood at best. When we understand in its simplest terms that we can only do what Jesus does through us, we've taken the first step in realigning a God-centered perception of ourselves.

When I was growing up, my family raised horses. My dad always kept a day job (or night job, you might say with it being shift work), but raising horses was a thriving family enterprise. We frequently made trips around our part of the southeastern US hauling horses to sales or shows.

I'll never forget one particular trip. I was in high school, but Dad let me skip a Friday to help him take a load of horses on a trip to Mississippi. He worked all night, loaded the horses when he got in from the plant, and off we went. Since he was coming off a twelve-hour shift, he had me take the wheel, and he crawled in the backseat to get some sleep.

This was normal for us, but what I remember that day was that as a car passed in the left lane, the passenger caught my attention. So you have to get the picture: I'm a sixteen-year-old girl behind the wheel of a one-ton dually truck hooked to a twenty-two-foot five-horse trailer headed north on I-55. The passing car sees this and only this and throws me a giant thumbs-up with both hands. You'd have thought I just passed the bar exam from his over-the-top-proud thumbs-upping. I'm not talking about a casual wave—I mean a stand-on-the-brakes move to get beside me and the exuberance of a skilled groupie waving and congratulating me as though trailer-hauling were an Olympic-level feat. I waved back, and they beamed and shot on past me.

I carelessly took some immature level of pride in the story and told it to others. But I got to thinking about it later, and the absurdity struck me. The whole kicker was that Dad was in the backseat the whole time. It was his truck, his horses he had loaded, and it was he who'd taught me to drive. I had the confidence to haul the trailer simply because I knew he was inches away and could take over at a moment's notice.

Friends, God calls us to do some uncomfortable things. And from the outside it may look overwhelming or even ridiculous. But if you remember it's your Father who's called you and that He is with you, showing you how to take each next step, it's not really you who's doing it anyway.

QUESTIONS FOR REFLECTION

- Have you found yourself doubting God can use you?
- Have you ever used any of the following as an excuse for why you are not worthy of being loved, called, and used by God?
  - ° Sins from the past
  - ° Lack of education
  - ° Family background
  - ° Lack of experience or abilities
  - ° [Something else plaguing you]
- What can you do to combat this thinking?

PRAYER

Jesus, I see myself for what I am. I confess my need for You today and every day. I thank You for the things in my life that make me realize my need for You. I take hope today in the knowledge that Your strength is made perfect in my weakness. I am asking you to take every weakness, fault, failure, frailty, and every other problem in my life that makes me feel like a puny grasshopper and turn me into one redeemed grasshopper among many in a mighty army You can use for Your glory.

GOD LOVES GRASSHOPPERS

have the most brilliant nephews and nieces on the planet. I am sorry if you thought your family members were in the running; mine have secured the top prize soundly. I was back home and in church with my beautiful niece when she was five. During the altar service I pulled her over to sit with me and prayed sincerely that God would keep her near the cross. After my prayer I looked at her with profound conviction and enunciated with deep sincerity, "Hailey, Jesus loves you very much!"

I'll never forget what happened next. She tilted her head to look at me in a manner reserved for those who need things explained slowly, and replied as matter of factly as if she were spelling her name, which she's very good at, "I know."

I did not let her see me chuckle, but several things became clear instantly. Mom, Dad, and the Sunday school team had done such a good job with her, she was left wondering how someone at my age had just figured out that Jesus loves us. That issue is already locked in her mind as an absolute.

Have you ever wondered when you realized that Jesus loved you? I hope it was a beautiful reality from your childhood. But unfortunately I still find many people far along in the journey of life who have not yet grasped this point.

Insecure young people come from insecure older people. It may be the result of the fact that mindsets and concepts of identity and worth are often inherited. Psychologists get paid billions of dollars each year to help adults recover from parents' words that left nearly irreparable damage.

It's no small surprise the Israelites had insecurities; Daddy Moses was a poster child for insecurities. It was inevitable really. When you're born during an era when the pharaoh says all boys must be killed, it's not the most nurturing environment. Add to that living in foster care—albeit in nice digs—after being in hiding for your debut in the world. Moses was not exactly the textbook case for an ideal home life.

So when God got Moses' attention with the burning bush, Moses gave wrong answers. Moses worried the people wouldn't listen to him—not exactly the kinds of leadership attributes described in the latest Ken Blanchard books. Even after God showed His miraculous power with the rod-snake incident, Moses told God he wasn't good with words and tried to bow out. For all of these identity-questioning responses, Scripture records that "the anger of the Lord was kindled against Moses" (Exodus 4:14). The idea of an all-powerful God being angry with me is a bit unnerving. You would think Moses would want to conquer this insecurity thing.

Fast-forward a few years later to the infamous grasshopper scene with the spies, and God's response to the spies' self-diagnosis is not altogether different from his ire at Moses. After working all day to convince their neighbors of the impossibility of God's promise, the group spent the night crying and wailing. The subtle whispers of "we'll be killed" turned to "maybe we should go back to Egypt" and by morning, the rioters were plotting to pick a new leader (Numbers 14:1–4).

Misunderstanding who you are as a child of God has disastrous ripple effects. Fear and insecurity from skewed vision breeds defeatist tendencies including mistrust and often outright rebellion against leaders and even God Himself. And I think we all know how God feels about rebellion. (Start with I Samuel 15 if you your memory is fuzzy.)

Picture the chaos of the scene—Moses and Aaron falling on their faces in yet another emergency session of Congress, as it were, and Joshua and Caleb ripping their clothes in righteous indignation and shame over their turntail comrades. It escalated to talk of stoning, and just as it seemed it would take full riot gear and a SWAT team to rescue the good guys, God showed up, and He was not happy (Numbers 14:10).

Perhaps some portions of Scripture require careful, sensitive reading with detailed study of the original biblical languages to understand the nuances at work in the text. Numbers 14:12 is no such passage. God made Himself very clear: He would simply kill all the grasshoppers and start over with Moses to make a new nation.

It's a terrorizing, radical plan that doesn't mesh well with the gentle Jesus image we've explained to a sensitive twenty-first century audience. But God feels strongly about how we treat Him, His promises, ourselves, and one another. Verse 12 paints a crystal-clear picture: when the spies said, "Those other guys are big and we are puny grasshoppers," God heard, "After everything You've done for us from the plagues to the Red Sea to the manna, we still don't think You can take care of us. We reject Your call to rise up and be Your warriors."

Have you ever overheard a family member taking a potshot at you? Maybe your daughter is in ninth grade and in the last three years you've suddenly become very, very uncool (don't worry—the process will magically reverse itself in about ten to fifteen years). Perhaps she has a sleepover and you overhear her complaining that you are out of touch or [fill in descriptive label]. Even if you know it's just a phase, it still probably hurts. This metaphor breaks down quickly when we apply it to God because He's not an insecure human and He doesn't need our affirmation. Yet He does emote a strong response and, at least from this account, He apparently gets angry when we reject Him and the things He wants to do in our lives.

God doesn't characterize defeatist thinking very fondly:

- Scripture records the spies gave "a bad report"—also described as "evil" in some translations (Numbers 13:30).
- God said the people treated Him with contempt (Numbers 14:23).
- God said the spies "despised" the land He promised (Numbers 14:31).
- God declared the people would face the consequences of their behavior (Numbers 14:34).
- God said the people were an "evil congregation who are gathered together against Me" (Numbers 14:35).
- God classified the people's actions as "turn[ing] away from the LORD" (Numbers 14:43).

It doesn't take a very religious person to want to avoid such a list. However, have you ever stopped to question why this was such a big deal to God? The spies' report was not originally untrue. Was it a big deal that they were scared or even that they underestimated God? After all . . . He's God. Why does He care about what we think?

To be sure, God does not have an identity problem. He tells and shows exactly what He is capable of, and it's a hide-your-eyes-it's-too-overwhelming kind of thing when He chooses to unleash His glory. And yet He doesn't want you to have an identity problem either. We are made in His image and so closely connected to Him that any self-loathing is also a slam at Him.

Again the metaphor fails to do justice, but if your kid has your curly hair and is always complaining about how ugly it is and how he hates it, it's hard not to connect the dots and infer what he thinks about your wavy locks.

Failing to take God at His Word and see ourselves as His chosen vessel is a way of treating Him contemptuously. It discredits everything He has already done in our lives and tells Him we have no faith in His future provision.

Some of you are thinking, "Wait a second, God was mad because they didn't trust Him and believe He would deliver them from the giants. What does that have to do with identity? Are you saying that someone with low self-esteem or a poor self-image is sinning?" Not necessarily. What I am saying is that self-image problems for Christians are not isolated because our identity as a child of God should be the most fundamental element of what makes you you. To let thoughts of your perceived flaws turn into self-abuse ignores the fact that you are His precious child. The certainty that you are so loved by God He gave Himself for you should be enough to rattle you when you're tempted to wander down dangerous roads of thinking you're worthless or unloved.

When you say "I am so stupid" or "I am an idiot" or "loser" or whatever your disparaging word of choice, you are slandering the apex of God's creation. I know we all make mistakes and get frustrated with ourselves from time to time, but when we choose to live with the delusion that we are not valuable, meaningful vessels of worth, we have slandered God's highest creative work. Furthermore, I can't fathom how a God who said it's better to drown than hurt a child and who said loving your neighbor is right up there with loving God Himself would be okay with you shredding yourself with your words. If He wouldn't want you to disrespect someone else in word or deed (and if you wouldn't do it either), don't treat yourself with such degradation.

Maybe we Christians have been guilty of turning the simple phrase into a cliché or somehow sucking the power out of these words, but let me say it again: God loves you. No other sentence ever uttered or etched competes or compares. He loves you. He doesn't love you because you're cute or smart or a hard worker or you pray a lot or you have a talent very few people have or because He feels sorry for you or . . . or . . . or . . . . He loves you because you are His. He loves you so much that making the galaxies and the seasons and the majestic Alps and the mesmerizing Caribbean and the fascinating way giraffes yawn and hummingbirds hover and lions shred prey was not enough. He wanted to make you to love.

It may seem elementary, but the number of people who can't get their heads around the fact that He loves us is staggering. It's a simple concept that we complicate. I wish there were a metaphor that made it easy for people to accept that God really does love them. But any metaphor subtracts from what comes down to a simple acceptance of ultimate, unconditional love. If you're struggling with that acceptance, bury yourself in these Scriptures. Print them out and paste them all over your house; memorize them and make it a point to say them daily. Find a way to saturate your mind with these life-giving Words:

> "How precious also are Your thoughts to me, O God! How great is the sum of them! If I should count them, they would be more in number than the sand" (Psalm 139:17–18).

"For God so loved the world that He gave His only begotten Son" (John 3:16).

"Behold what manner of love the Father has bestowed on us, that we should be called children of God!" (I John 3:1).

Every time you say with your words, thoughts, or actions that you are too [fill in the blank with negative label], you're doing so without the sanction of the One who loves you infinitely. Mitchell Bland, an Apostolic counselor and pastor, put it this way: "It's so sad that people live with the perception that they are not good enough to be accepted by the very God who made them."[1] Do you have your flaws? Yes. Until this vapor called life passes, we all will. Is His love a license to ignore flaws and not look to Him for help in growing through them? No. But His love is the motivation to look at ourselves through a godly lens and see ourselves as He sees us. The first and fundamental step of establishing or realigning your God-ordained identity is to accept that God loves you.

QUESTIONS FOR REFLECTION

- Have you found yourself obsessed with your personal flaws?
- Do you have trouble believing God loves you?
- Have you found yourself trying to do things to earn God's love?
- Is it possible God is disappointed with your hesitation to trust Him for His promises or your constant belittling of yourself?
- How can you realign your thinking with the realization that God loves you?

PRAYER

Jesus, thank You for loving me. I am saying the words with my mouth; help me to believe it with my head and my heart. Your love is what gives my life meaning. Because You love me, I can start on the path to seeing myself as worthwhile since I am loved by You. Help me start that journey.

CHAPTER 5

HANDMADE GRASSHOPPERS

Perception is a funny thing. You've probably heard it said that a person's perception is her reality. I never knew how powerful that tendency was until a few years ago on the golf course. As a female über-amateur golfer, I am usually the hold-up on the course, but on one particular afternoon, a friend and I spent the day behind a painfully slow Calorie Crusher (my term for those warriors who walk the course). We teed off on an elevated par three and knocked it onto the green. My friend pulled off a birdie while I proudly two-putted for par.

Sitting in the cart waiting for the Calorie Crusher to zig zag across the next fairway, the foursome behind us pulled up with Captain Mediocre Golfer and what I presumed to be his grand-children in tow. He slammed the brake of the cart, threw a thumb back at the par three they'd just finished after us, and exclaimed, "Wow, I thought you were guys on that last hole!"

I almost offered to buy Captain Mediocre Golfer a steak dinner then and there. My golfing buddy, however, almost throat-punched him. I heard, "You play some great golf with the driving distance of a male golfer." I'm not sure what my friend heard, but it was not flattering. The man went on to compliment us on our golf, but his comment revealed gaping differences in our perception.

We both had hearing levels that fall within normal ranges. The man said the same words to both of us. But we each heard two vastly different things based on our prior experiences, our scopes of reference, and what we wanted to hear.

The term *handmade* reveals biases as well. Dolly Parton captured this sentiment with her famous autobiographical song of a coat her mother made with fabric scraps because they were too poor to afford cloth from a single bolt. Her mother's story that the coat was special like Joseph's made young Dolly take pride in the coat until she got to school and the little jerks in her class picked on her for it being obviously handmade from scraps.

For many people, something being handmade implies custom-crafted quality fashioned with care. For others it connotes something home-grown and not produced with the same quality standards as its professionally manufactured counterparts. You'd think having a handmade dress from Mom would be a treasure, but every spring little girls throw crying fits of protest as they push back against the new Easter dress Mom carefully and lovingly sewed.

Adam and Eve could relate. They were custom crafted by the Master Artisan, and they were made in His image. And yet these original grasshoppers still overlooked the treasure they were to God and the treasure they had in being in such a special relationship with God.

Indeed, understanding the origins of identity problems requires a look back at Creation itself.[1] Try to think about things from God's perspective. He had fashioned a planet that is as fascinating as it is beautiful. He had made animals of sweeping diversity. And then He made a human. He made that human with His own hands and His own breath, reaching down and picking up the very dust of the earth in a delicate and potent act. Consider it: humans are God's handmade creation, fashioned proudly and lovingly by a perfect God who looked at His craftsmanship and declared in His Word, "it was very good" (Genesis 1:31).

Study of the Hebrew syntax suggests this act of creation involved God's handmade craftsmanship. The verb *yatsar* indicates forming or fashioning an object and is used also to speak of human potters molding clay vessels.[2] This pottery connection should be familiar to the student of Scripture who remembers God telling Jeremiah to go the potter's house and there comparing the potter's work to what He would do with the people of Israel (Jeremiah 18:1–11). Isaiah said, "We are the clay, and You our potter; And all we are the work of Your hand" (Isaiah 64:8). This extended metaphor speaks of God's work being directly involved in the creation of humanity.

Notice also that not only are people handcrafted by God, but the breath of God gave Adam life. That breath that made Adam a living soul is significant.

> This single act of special creation, God breathing into man "the breath of life," distinguished humanity from all other creatures. We share with the animals a biological shell composed, in our case, of bone, organs, muscle, fat, and skin. In truth, we fall short in direct comparison to the strictly biological features of some animals. Who would compete in beauty with a splashy macaw or even a lowly luna moth? A horse easily outruns us, a hawk sees far better, a dog detects odors and sounds imperceptible to us. The total sum

of our sheer physical qualities is no more godlike than a cat's.

And yet, *we* are made in the image of God. For us, the shell of skin and muscle and bones serves as a vessel, a repository for His image. We can comprehend and even convey something of the creator.[3]

The authors go on to stress that humans are immortal. When we speak of our souls living on for eternity somewhere, we are exercising a faith in the special way in which God made us—in a realm different from any other creature.

It is not just a matter of being superior to an animal that makes our creation significant. The process by which we were created is special. Systematic theologian Robert Peterson puts it this way, "There is an intimacy present in God's creation of His highest creature—humanity—that is lacking in the creation of the animals. . . . Our being made from dust speaks to our humble origins and our utter dependence upon our creator for life and breath."[4] Simply put, not only do we know from Scripture that God loves us, but the intimate act of creation shows that from the beginning of time, God made us to be His beloved possession.

God did more than craft us by hand; He made us in His own image. Genesis 5:1–2, 9:6, and James 3:9 reiterate this critical detail of Creation. Yet do we know what it means to be made in the image of God? The implication is that something in us or about us connects to and reflects God. And that is a big deal. So much so, that it prompted a warning about murder—taking life bears special consequences since humans are made in God's image (Genesis 9:6).

Do we look like God in our physical attributes? I'll not venture to dismiss or speculate; we'll see soon enough when we behold

Him. What I do believe is that there is something very special and valuable about every human being. No life—no matter the labels or physical and mental condition—is without worth; we are fashioned after God.

Beyond physical attributes, what could being made in God's image mean? What are the implications? In an unpublished paper, Everett Gossard considered the topic and reminded us to approach the issue with a few foundational truths in mind:

> First, that humanity, as the creation in the image of God, is a very special thing, considerably higher up in the created order as opposed, to say, animals. Secondly, from the intention of God, humanity was meant to be perfect and without sin. One cannot make an argument for original sin without grappling with the problem of "How could that be possible if humanity was created in the image of God?"[5] Third, God's creation is at essence, good. Certainly, the scripture affirms that there is none righteous, no not one, but from the creation itself, God intended for humanity to be righteous.[6]

Gossard's final point should not be glossed over. We must approach study of being made in God's image with a recognition that God's creation is good and He intended good things for us.

Theologians have invested millions of hours of study and reams of paper to articulate theories of substantive, relational, and functional ways in which humanity is made in the image of God.[7] That is to say, do we reflect His likeness in our inherent nature (substantive), in our relationships (relational), or the roles we carry out (functional)? I was always one to fall for the "d - all of the above" answer on the multiple choice test, so I'm prone to consider a combination of these theories. I hope when I work, I reflect a God who was Himself first described in Scripture at work on Creation. When I build relationships of trust, compassion, and integrity, I hope I reflect the nature of Jesus Christ. And I hope I treat my body and respect myself in a way that honors being made in the image of God.

However, when we look back to the original passage of Creation, the text closely links the authoritative function of Adam with being made in the image of God, and the account of life in the Garden suggests an intimacy of relationship with God. In Genesis 1:26 God announced His plan to make humanity in His image and "let them have dominion" over the animals. In Genesis 1:27–28, after creating humanity in His image, God immediately blessed them and gave them the commands to subdue and have dominion over the rest of Creation. Scripture further details Adam's responsibility to dress and keep the Garden and name the animals (Genesis 2:15–20). These functions of governing and stewarding Creation were meant to be accomplished in partnership with God. Furthermore, Genesis 3:8 suggests God walked with Adam and Eve, an ongoing relationship of harmony and perfect communion.

This drive for relationship is so powerful it has affected the course of human history. For thousands of years religions have looked for ways to explain the connection between humanity and deity. Many religious teachers would suggest that a mere mortal human could not approach God. Some religions even went to the extent of creating intermediaries or lesser gods they thought could be approached by humans. All of these theological developments were in response to the desire to understand how humanity can relate to God, and yet they overlooked the basic starting point of creation—the truth that God made people and enjoyed fellowship with them.[8]

Yet all of this was not good enough for the original grasshoppers. Adam and Eve traded the splendor of being made in God's image—living in perfect relationship with God and governing His creation—for the counterfeit promise of knowledge.

The fall of the original grasshoppers reveals the danger we still face in defining our identity without including our relationship with God in the equation. Grasshoppers who cannot be satisfied with who God made them to be look for bigger, better, and more to their own demise. In Eve's case, she succumbed when she perceived the tree was "pleasant to the eyes, and a tree desirable to make one wise" (Genesis 3:6). Only someone insecure in her identity as a handmade child of God could be tempted by one tree when she had her pick of the whole Garden. Her temptation emphasizes why we must recognize insecure thinking for what it is and banish it from our thought life; when we are not secure in our relationship with God and in the authority He has given us as His children, we open ourselves to lies of the enemy and carnal temptations that appeal to our insatiable hunger for more, bigger, and better.

In the original grasshoppers' fall, we also learn much about being made in the image of God from what was lost. Leaving the majestic Garden and being cursed with work and pain were not the worst calamities of the Fall. The relational aspect of being in God's presence was fractured, and that was the greatest loss of all. Reconciling the failing of the first Adam took the work of the second Adam, Jesus:

> And so it is written, "The first man Adam became a living being." The last Adam became a life-giving spirit. However, the spiritual is not first, but the natural, and afterward the spiritual. The first man was of the earth, made of dust; the second

Man is the Lord from heaven. As was the man of dust, so also are those who are made of dust; and as is the heavenly Man, so also are those who are heavenly. And as we have borne the image of the man of dust, we shall also bear the image of the heavenly Man (I Corinthians 15:45–49).

Though the Fall saw a loss of innocence and a break in the perfect communion God wanted with us, that image of God we were endowed with was not completely revoked. Because of the revelation of the oneness of God and our understanding that Jesus is the image of the invisible God (Colossians 1:15) and that His redemptive act brings us into relationship with Him so "we shall also bear the image of the heavenly Man," hope is not lost! While we are made in the image of God and have innate worth simply as His children, we are conformed to His image when we are reborn and enter a covenant relationship with Jesus Christ (Romans 8:29; Colossians 3:9–10): "He made us in His image, and He completes our likeness in His image spiritually when we are born again of His Spirit."[9] That promise of hope still extends to all of humanity (Acts 2:38–39). Salvation is not just about escaping condemnation but about becoming who God called us to be.

Being made in God's image is not a fact existing in a vacuum without contemporary applications. We recognize that part of being made in His image included having dominion. We had it in the Garden, and we'll have it when we rule and reign with Him in eternity. Yet we can also have authority and be empowered in this life to be "more than conquerors" (Romans 8:37) when we're filled with His Spirit.

Our theological clarity on being made in the image of God is critical. God's handmade creations are not worthless or pitiable. That's where the spies in Numbers 13 went wrong. They didn't understand their God-connection. The looked at their problem with the overgrown varsity football team as something they had to solve alone, and under the circumstances, absolutely they were puny freshmen destined to be stuffed in a locker. What they didn't see was that they were really being called into a new level of identity and authority as warriors instead of wanderers.

We must understand God loves us. Then we must understand He handcrafted us in His own image. Our insecurities and self-loathing evaporate in the richness of that reality.

Maybe we haven't thought long enough and hard enough about what it means to be made in His likeness. Vestal Goodman put it awfully succinctly when she sang, "[I was] created in His image, for I was born to serve the Lord."[10] What we know is that humanity was originally created in God's image and if we are to reign with Him in eternity, we must be conformed to His image.

In our Western minds we would like to draw a flowchart and a timeline for precisely what God intended when He made us in His likeness and exactly how that image is realigned with redemption. I have no such flowchart. What we can establish from the account of Scripture is that God designed us with a special divine imprint. It wasn't a passing detail of the Genesis record to say we were formed in His likeness; that is sufficient evidence to impress on us that we are precious to God.

Sadly the reality is many people are filled with self-loathing. Theologians Gordon Lewis and Bruce Demarest assert, "Apparently few people are totally satisfied with their bodies. Most of us feel some physical limitations in appearance or in coordination of athletic, musical, or artistic talents."[11] While in some degree of moderation it can be natural to critique certain parts of our physical body, it is imperative we recognize we are creations of God. In John 2:14–16 Jesus put a grade-A smackdown on people who were mistreating the Temple building. Think then of His reaction when He sees His children destroying their human bodies: "Our flesh matters just like our spirit matters. Our fleshly bodies house the Spirit and presence of God. . . . It matters to God what you do with your body."[12] It could be argued that cutting your body whether for release of internal pain or to achieve unattainable standards of beauty is a lack of understanding your self-worth. In either case I beg you to allow someone you trust in your life to step in and help you find healing in Jesus. If you are struggling with an eating disorder of any kind, whether it's intemperate eating, bulimia, anorexia, or any number of issues, God loves you and wants to help you find peace with the way He has made you. He loves you so much that He calls people to professional ministries who can help you with any of these issues.

The testimony of Scripture establishes that His fingerprint on us was intentional and significant. Ephesians 2:10 reminds us, "For we are His workmanship, created in Christ Jesus for good works, which God prepared beforehand that we should walk in them." We are His custom-crafted treasures, and there's nothing insignificant about that.

QUESTIONS FOR REFLECTION

- Does your relationship with God reflect a desire for communing with Him?
- Does your lifestyle reflect and honor the fact that you were handcrafted in His likeness?
- Do you struggle with negative thoughts about your body? How should the understanding that you were made in God's image recalibrate your thinking?
- Are you doing something to damage your body? Who in your life do you trust to talk to for help? Will you commit to this process of accountability and healing?

PRAYER

Father, when I am honest with myself and You, I confess that I often lose sight of the fact that I was handcrafted by You in Your image. I want to pursue the close relationship with You that You desire. Help me, Jesus, to realign my life and my priorities to make my relationship with You the source of my identity. I accept that You make good things and You love me and think good thoughts toward me. Thank you for Your love, Jesus.

CHAPTER 6

GRASSHOPPERS WITH SKIN

When I was six, my dad bought a bay quarter horse stallion that was at once majestic and terrifying. An own son of the legendary sire Impressive, Adonis (his registered name) was unlike any horse we ever owned. He had the strength of a draft horse. My dad dallied railroad crossties to the saddlehorn, and Adonis ran up and down the pasture towing them for exercise.

Many stallions are naturally aggressive and territorial, but Adonis made the brutest of them look like amateurs. As our barn cats walked across the top of the walls to Adonis's stall, some eight feet high, Adonis would periodically pick up a cat in his enormous jaws, dangle her in mid-air (I suppose to remind her she was trespassing) and when bored with the activity, deposit her back on the wall.

We had one frequent visitor to the barn named Michael. Michael loved Adonis, but he was terrified of him. The amazing part was that Adonis knew it. Other visitors to the barn could come and go and never merit so much as a semi-interested snort from Adonis, but when Michael rounded the corner to the barn, Adonis turned into the worst possible version of himself. He would pin his ears to his neck, bare his teeth, charge from the back of the stall, and slam into the metal grate, snorting and pawing.

Without fail, Michael would careen back against the wall on the other side of the alleyway, terror in his eyes. Yet within milliseconds, Michael's fear would morph into adoration, and he'd utter some version of, "Wow, what a horse!"

I remember as a kid not knowing what to think of Adonis. He was beautiful and strong, but I saw what a monster he could be enough to know to be afraid of him too. Unlike Michael in his state of unwavering devotion, I was perplexed. Was Adonis a good horse or a bad horse?

Sometimes I wonder if contemporary Christianity has done a disservice in the way we've taught believers to think about human nature. We have a world culture that has chosen to believe humanity is innately good and that if we'll be the best version of ourselves, we'll be good individuals and that will transcend into better and better communities. I call these people the Michaels of life. They are being played by the selfishness and depravity of our culture and are too blinded to see the seed of evil within humanity and the decline of morality and unrighteousness in our world for what it is.

Yet perhaps the church is not perfect in this equation either. In recognizing the potential for evil and the inclination toward unrighteousness, have we been too quick to presume the worst in human nature and label humans broadly as "bad?" Maybe.

The Corinthian church ran into some of these issues. As a major seaport for the Aegean and Adriatic Seas, the people of Corinth were exposed to a wide array of philosophies and ideologies, some of which contradicted the teachings of Jesus Christ. One such idea was that the physical body was bad. This originated from Greek dualist philosophy that separated physical and spiritual components. The Gnostics were so affected by these dualistic theories that they rejected the Incarnation on the grounds that a holy God could not inhabit a human (bad) body. Many Corinthians had recognized the value of spirituality, which was good, but conversely they assumed everything about the physical person was bad. Consequently, many believers were careless with how they treated their bodies or even veered to the extreme of asceticism, which involved punishing and mutilating their bodies. (See also Colossians 2:23.)

Paul corrected this teaching in I Corinthians 6. Though in the context of guidelines for sexuality, Paul expounded on the value of our bodies: "They were made for the Lord, and the Lord cares about our bodies" (I Corinthians 6:13, NLT). Paul went on to clarify with two verses that Apostolics love to preach: "What? know ye not that your body is the temple of the Holy Ghost which is in you, which ye have of God, and ye are not your own? For ye are bought with a price: therefore glorify God in your body, and in your spirit, which are God's" (I Corinthians 6:19–20, KJV). These verses are more than a reminder for practical holiness application, though that is important. These verses should also be a mantra for understanding how to view our whole person. Clearly our physical bodies were made by God (in His image) and were meant to be part of what makes us us.

I love Dottie Rambo and try to strum my guitar and warble her songs with the best of them, but Dottie tangled with theology and got tripped up. In this instance, she went Greek on us when she penned, "This house of clay is but a prison, bars of bone hold my soul."[1] I understand the sentiment: we want to be in Heaven so much sometimes it feels like we are being caged by our bodies and the physical connection to this temporal world (especially on tax day and driver's license renewal day). But to classify the body God handcrafted (in His image) as a cage or prison overlooks Paul's teaching that our body was made by God to glorify Him.

There is a difference between what we possess and what is part of our identity.

Wrong thinking: "I am a soul and I have a body. [The soul is the real me.]"

Biblical reality: Humans exist as body, soul, and spirit. You cannot take apart who we are and draw strong lines between these elements. The body was made by God, He does all things well, and so the body is good.

So we were made by God with a fleshly body that is good, but what do we do with Scriptures that talk about crucifying the flesh? In fact, many of us could easily rattle off a dozen or so Scripture verses that suggest troublesome human nature and speak of resident evil in our flesh. What gives?

One of the first passages we should address is Romans 7:14–25. In the larger context, Paul was establishing the need for Jesus Christ's atoning work at Calvary. When Paul said there was no good thing in him (verse 18), notice the parenthetical interruption he used to clarify his own statement. It's not that he as a whole person is not good, but his "flesh" is not good. That sounds like we're back to square one since we just established that our bodies are created by God and are good. However, there is a nuance from the Greek language lost in translation that holds the key to understanding this passage and others like it in light of I Corinthians 6 and the understanding that our bodies are gifts from God.

Two related nouns were used frequently in the New Testament:

English	Greek
body	*soma*
flesh	*sarx*

In English, the words *body* and *flesh* have similar meanings but in Greek, *soma* and *sarx* have distinct meanings. *Soma* was about the church body, and it was not a bad term. Scripture even uses the metaphor of a body to describe God's people (I Corinthians 12). However, *sarx* meant something altogether different; it indicated our sinful nature. When a Greek writer spoke of skin and toenails, he used *soma*. When he indicated the dependence on the corruptible flesh and that which is allied against God, he used *sarx*.[2]

When Paul talked about the "flesh," he was talking about our corruptible and decaying nature. Even though the body is made by God, it is corruptible because we live in a fallen world and we have a flesh that will at some point decay. Moreover, each of us must cope with our human tendency to sin.

So are human beings naturally good or naturally bad? The answer is another "d - all of the above." We need to affirm the goodness of God's creation and that God is a perfect Creator. The fact that we have a physical body and funny-looking elbows and big toes is not bad; that part of us will decay physically, but it is not a source of wickedness. In fact, our bodies are not at war with our spirits. But our sinful nature is at war against the Spirit of God and what He wants to do in our lives. That is the issue.

When Paul bemoaned that there was nothing good in his flesh, his sinful nature, he recognized that without daily surrender to let the Spirit of the Lord have dominance in his life, that depraved evil nature would derail the good things of God (Romans 7:18). "And those who are Christ's have crucified the flesh with its passions and desires" (Galatians 5:24). That choice—every day resisting selfish, unrighteous impulses and instead pursuing the reign of the Holy Ghost in our lives—is what gives us our identity. Without God we are grasshoppers too small and too weak to fight off the sin nature. But a God-called man or woman who allows the

Holy Ghost to reign and be the source of his or her identity does not have to live captive to sin. Yes, we will daily confront that sin nature, but because we allow God to transform us into His image, our identity and our future will be triumphant: "There is therefore now no condemnation to those who are in Christ Jesus, who do not walk according to the flesh, but according to the Spirit. For the law of the Spirit of life in Christ Jesus has made me free from the law of sin and death" (Romans 8:1–2).

QUESTIONS FOR REFLECTION

- Can you relate to Paul's struggle with the selfishness of his sinful nature (*sarx*)?
- What patterns of destructive, selfish impulses (*sarx*) have you identified in your life?
- What can you do in response?

PRAYER

Father, I thank You that I am fearfully and wonderfully made. I know that You make good things, and I dedicate my body to Your service and seek Your help in treating it as Your temple. I also recognize there is a selfish nature in me, and today I ask for Your help—Your grace and strength—to deal with the daily struggle of my selfish, destructive impulses. Cover me in Your blood and keep me from evil. Thank You for Your mercy!

CHAPTER 7

FALLEN GRASSHOPPERS

We didn't spend a lot of time in the principal's office in our family. Our parents had gone to the school and told all our teachers if we gave any trouble to discipline us and then call them and they would one-up it at home that night. I never thought for a second of calling their bluff. I knew they were dead serious.

So when my Dad told me one day on the way home from school that the principal had called, I was decidedly panic-stricken. I knew exactly why she'd called.

Joe Montana and Jerry Rice were idols to our fifth-grade class. In actuality, that's not much of an exaggeration. Every recess, PE class, and after-school break centered on enacting the latest Montana-Rice touchdown pass.

My Uncle Aubrey close-cropped the front lawn of the school to a length we determined was an ideal gridiron. When we decided the teachers weren't looking, we switched from flag to tackle football on cue. To navigate the inevitable arguments over out-of-bounds close calls, we decided to use the sidewalk and brick columns that bordered the east end of the lawn as the home team's end zone. (Somehow at age ten it seemed perfectly logical to run the length of the field headlong into concrete and brick.)

On that fateful day, however, Stephen tackled my kid brother and knocked him right into one of the brick columns. I levied an instant and no doubt astute judgment that Stephen's hit had been unnecessary roughness. Confidently acting as both referee and NFL players' safety commissioner, I brought justice to bear by socking Stephen right in the gut.

Sure enough, Stephen had ratted me out and the principal had called. The funny part is, I had been confident that when I explained how I had represented the family, my Dad would understand, yea, would be proud I had carried out sure and swift justice. But even as the words tumbled out, my case unraveled. My Dad's advice on handling our anger landed on ears already convicted by the heaviness of sin.

Many good people can burn through a number of cups of coffee debating whether humans are innately sinful or if humans are born with a proclivity to sin. If those two things sound the same, you're in good company. That's what I thought too. After wading through the theological discussion, I think the central question can be translated like this: do we sin because we're sinners or are we sinners because we sin? I have to be honest with you. The simplified version trips me up about as much as the first. We can catch ourselves in a theological loop here and chase our tails. While I'm glad there are people who feel they've figured it out and can explain it, the bottom line is that in either case, "all have sinned and fall short of the glory of God" (Romans 3:23).

I will admit that it took me a long time to get my head around that as a kid. Statements like "we're all born into sin" and "all sins are equal" did not logically compute. Still a part of me as a capitalist-loving, free-enterprising North American strains at the theology wrapped up in all of this talk about sin. The truth, however, is that while there are nuances, we must accept the reality that at our base nature (*sarx*), we will sin and we must have the work of Calvary to atone for our sin.

I don't know if I slugged Stephen because I had a proclivity or because I was a sinner, but I know this much: everything in me knotted up and socked him with an exhilaration that was scary. I was every bit prepared to justify it, and I was every bit convicted when my sin was brought to light.

Grasshoppers sin. We can resist the language because it's not popular in a world that thinks Christians are wound too tight, but that doesn't change the reality of our fallen nature that is susceptible to temptation and susceptible to sin.

There must be an acceptance of the lethal reality of sin or else we minimize the need for God's grace and atonement. If humanity is not innately sinful, then theoretically humans could live above sin by mere behavioral modification. We could begin our lives in innocence and, much like success in the Old Covenant would have required, attempt to avoid sinful conduct. However, we must acknowledge that within us is a sinful nature and no one ever was successful in living without sin under the Old Covenant.

This book rests on the scriptural foundation that we are made in the image of God. When you realize that Jesus came to earth in fully human form and was Himself tempted, it gives perspective to our temptations. Of course we are going to be tempted. It is part and parcel of having blood pump through our body. No one knew this reality of temptation better than the men and women of the Bible. We sometimes remember them as the one-dimensional cut-outs on the flannelgraph without the same compulsions and obsessions you and I have. But they were 100 percent human.

Compare the polar opposites of David and Goliath and you'll easily see the stark contrasts. It's easy to beat up on that ungodly heathen giant who dared to blaspheme God. But what about other men from the Bible who had less of an excuse to fail?

Let's do something different and look at David in comparison to Samson:

David	Samson
• Chosen and anointed by God	• Chosen and anointed by God
• Gifted with special abilities	• Gifted with special abilities
• Specially directed in his youth to fight the Philistines	• Specially directed in his youth to fight the Philistines
• Achieved feats of war and success as a young man	• Achieved feats of war and success as a young man
• Encountered temptation	• Encountered temptation

Trick questions aside, on paper these men's lives started out with striking parallels. They were called-out, gifted children of God with limitless potential in fulfilling special purposes for God's vision for His people. Yet our Sunday school classes could remind us that the conclusion to their stories ended differently. The factor? Their response when they encountered temptation.

It would have been nice to skip over this chapter. This is a book about identity and triumph and celebrating our Apostolic power as children of God. Who wants to talk about sin and temptation and the possibility—even assurance—that we will mess up? However, no talk about our identity as humans is complete without facing the inevitable: we will sin. We are grasshoppers (mortal, fallible creatures) who will face temptation, and there will be times we will sin. We must be confident in the Bible's plan for what we do when we sin and how we can find grace and forgiveness in Jesus Christ.

It's easy to beat up on Samson. If history is any indication, we usually don't take kindly to silver-spooned darlings who've been given every opportunity and blow it. After two visits from an angel promising her that her child would be special, Samson's mother went to great lengths to provide for the future of her baby boy. She had to make special dietary choices (Numbers 6:1–21) for herself and then see to it that little Samson grew up knowing not to cut his hair as a mark of consecration.

Yet we proceed from all the honorable sacrifices of Samson's parents in Judges 13 to Samson's first recorded acts in Judges 14. Disappointingly, Samson played loosely with his vow. He entered a vineyard, which would have been in opposition to his vow (Judges 14:5), and touched the lion's carcass, also violating his vow (Judges 14:8). With the terms of his vow being negotiable, it's no wonder Samson had trouble with inappropriate relationships. Still, his refusal to see through the ordeal with Delilah is mind-boggling.

While the writer of the Book of Judges does not offer commentary to explain Samson's choices, notably absent is any indication that Samson attempted to build a relationship with God. He only prayed twice—when he complained to God about being thirsty (Judges 15:18) and in his final moments when he sought revenge on his enemies (Judges 16:28). Samson was his own self-serving man, acting out of his own motivations—whatever they were. The record of the biblical text suggests that when Samson faced temptation, there was no preexisting relationship with God to guide him in responding to and dealing with his sinful nature.

And then there was David. First, he understood that God's power worked within him and it was his source of survival. From that conviction, David established a relationship with God. Prayer was a lifestyle for him. If the Book of Psalms is any indication, talking to God was as natural to him as breathing air.

How a man that passionate about prayer and worship could exercise such poor judgment as he did with Bathsheba only shows us how close sin lies to the door of all our hearts. Yet the point of sin's exposure in David's life marks the place where David and Samson's paths diverged.

First, David gave place for a minister of God in his life. When Nathan brought his sin to light, instead of turning a deaf ear or lashing out at Nathan, David listened to the voice of the prophet, humbled himself, and sought the Lord for forgiveness. Therein lies all the difference.

Yes, David was a worshiper. Yes, David spent time praying. Both of those things were valuable, but their value was only as meaningful as David's willingness to put them into practice in the moment of crisis. Though David failed to withstand temptation, when God in His mercy sent a minister to expose David's sin, David turned to God in repentance.

Lest I whitewash the perverseness of David's sin, let me point out what we often sanitize in our reading of Scripture. The king of a nation used his authority to take a woman from her home, abuse her, and have her husband killed to cover it up. When I work with young people who are struggling to believe God will forgive them of viewing pornography, I introduce them to David. When I see mothers who fear God is finished with a wayward child, allow me to point you to David. No one wants to be the cautionary tale, but David's repentance in II Samuel 11 is every bit as transforming for our lives as when he penned Psalm 23. I can trust in the mercy of a God who can forgive someone as wretched as David. You can too.

David called out to God in humility and the curse of sin was broken. Though he had to live with the scars and consequences of his past, the last chapter of his story is one of triumph. Samson, on the other hand, died with his enemy. No question remains that he was strong and competent, but his failure to acknowledge his strength as a gift of God, establish a relationship with God, and turn to God during times of temptation and personal mistakes sabotaged him.

One of the things the enemy seems to thrive on doing is magnifying our failures and past sins. This phenomenon ranges from the young adult who fears he can't find salvation because of the addiction he battles to the aspiring minister who fears she cannot be used by God because of a shameful past. The truth is that, yes, addictions and sin of any kind past or present can separate us from God and the intimacy He desires for our lives. All sin must be surrendered to Him—confessed and put under His precious blood forever with a sincere commitment to turn from it. Any other course of action such as denial, justification, bargaining, and so on, simply won't work.

So how do we shed the ways and mentality of the sin-plagued grasshopper? We go to God willing to change. Simple enough to prescribe and harder to carry out in real life. One thing that is crucial is to analyze your motives. Why are you doing, saying, and thinking whatever you are? This analysis needs to go beyond the surface and really get at the problem. Do you think what you are doing is not wrong? Do you think God doesn't see or care? Or do you think He makes exceptions for you? Or have you convinced yourself there's no way you can change?

Now instead of just focusing on the do's and don'ts to avoid the sin, focus on the heart issues. Fix those and the side effects cure themselves. The main fix, of course, is a surrender in God's presence. Understand you can't willpower yourself to perfect living. But you can determine to stay continually in His presence, and He can have dominion in your life.

Sin does have consequences, make no mistake. David and Paul had a lot more to live with than Jonah and Peter, but the adage you've heard before is true. Failure does not have to be final. Don't let your mistakes define your identity or dictate your future. God's love for you is bigger and His blood is more powerful than your worst mistakes. Choose to give them to Him and accept His help in overcoming them.

I am convinced the early church Apostolics were not perfect people, but they were faith-filled people. They believed on the threat of torture and death that God loved them and offered a radically new kind of life. That faith came from life-changing prayer meetings. Contemporary Apostolics have the audacity to take God at His Word when He told His followers they would do greater works (John 14:11–13). We believe we can experience the same intensity of the work of the Spirit today as the apostles did in the Book of Acts. Don't stoop to addictions that would hinder your ability to walk in the Spirit. Don't bow to temporal distractions when you could be climbing into the apostolic realm of the miraculous.

We are grasshoppers—fallible creatures, weak and doomed without God. There is nothing powerful about who we are except that God made us in His image, gifted us with talents, and gave us the freedom to choose the outcomes of our future. Wrapped up in all of that, however, is the reality that you will face the weight of your carnal nature every single day. Your temptation does not make you any less loved by God. Do you realize that Jesus Himself was tempted? To be a grasshopper is to be human, which means you will be tempted (James 1:14). Yet Scripture goes to great lengths to show us that God is merciful to forgive us if we will simply ask (I John 1:9). Furthermore, time in His presence brings us strength to overcome temptation and positions us in a place to be open to the way of escape He provides (I Corinthians 10:13).

QUESTIONS FOR REFLECTION

- On a scale of 1 to 10, how do you rate your commitment to turn to God for help with your temptations?
- What is your response when sin in your life is brought to light through the Word of God or a situation involving people?
- Today are there areas of your life where you need to repent and seek God's forgiveness? Will you commit to do that now?

PRAYER

Holy God, I am thankful that You remember my frame, that I am but dust. You have infinite mercy on me, and I am so humbled by Your love. I ask You today to once again cleanse me of my carnal attachments. I need Your mercy. I repent of every sin. I am sorry for how it separates me from You. I believe that You love me and forgive me. I thank You and praise You for the promise of Your grace and Your shed blood that eradicates my sins forever. That is the promise that gives me the hope to live, and I thank You!

CHAPTER 8

A GRASSHOPPER BY ANY OTHER NAME

When we were kids we lived for two things: (1) Fun Fair Park and (2) having company at our house. The latter was a more realistic hope. We loved having company for two reasons: (1) my mom, who can cook Paula Deen under a table, would put out a spread that was essentially a foreshadowing of the Marriage Supper of the Lamb and (2) at supper my dad would tell stories. We were mesmerized by them. Our favorites were Rudy the rodeo clown and his skunk and anything involving Mr. Bad John. We had heard these stories over and over, and anyone who says familiarity breeds contempt has never heard my dad tell a story. With every telling they became more endearing.

Here's hoping I will measure up to Dad's ability. I'm going to tell you a story that you've heard many times. It's important, though, that you hear it afresh.

The story is hard to start because God doesn't have a starting point. In the beginning, there was God, who has always been. But one time He decided that though He had angels that never stopped saying how great He was, He wanted something else. So He said, "Let there be [fill-in-the-blank]" and all of these things began poofing into existence—stars and the Sun and giant trees and microscopic plants and scary-looking fish and cuddly-looking walruses. And then when He had this new planet situated the way He wanted, He made a man and then a woman. These creatures were different than everything else He had made because He made them with His own hands instead of just ordering them to materialize into being. And He breathed into them a soul—a soul that would have the free choice to either roam around paradise in perfect communion with God or to choose an agenda where God's guidelines were negotiable. That man and woman picked door #2. The perfect paradise was no longer an option. Animals the man and woman had named and cared for had to die to cover up the man and woman's shame. And now that the people had chosen to negotiate with God about how to live in this world He had made for them, everything was a mess and their kids made fatal choices too.

But God was not taken by surprise and wringing His hands about what to do with these rebellious rascals. He came to earth Himself as a man, a lot like that first man He had created. But He was different, too, because He was fully God in human form. He healed people and raised the dead and transformed people's lives so they didn't want to do those things that put distance between them and Him. Those things God called sin. And though He hated sin, He took on Himself all of those sins and took the rap for all of human history. He was tortured to death to change the way humanity can approach God. Three days later He came back to life and told His close followers what had happened.

Slowly but surely they began to understand His master plan to put an end to this sin problem once and for all. And shortly after, some of His followers gathered to pray to God, thinking on all the words Jesus had told them. A noise like a hurricane sounded, and as the people prayed, they began to speak in languages they had never learned. People from town came to find out what the commotion was all about. One of the followers, Peter, had kind of made a mess of things during Jesus' arrest and execution. Peter had some faults, but He just kept trying to do what Jesus had taught them. And this day of the prayer meeting, He stood up and began to talk. He told the whole group they were responsible for killing Jesus. It was really uncomfortable at first. Then people began to get really upset because they knew, for all of Peter's flaws, he was right. With the burden of proof before them, these people began to feel the weight of sinful choices they had made. With heavy hearts they asked Peter and his cohorts what they could do to be saved. Peter told them to repent and be baptized in Jesus' name. He promised them that they would receive the Spirit of God (the Holy Ghost). That was the way to apply to their lives God's plan to have His own blood remove their sin (Acts 2:38). And for a couple thousand years now, people have been experiencing this same phenomenon to find an escape from the plague of sin.

Fallible grasshoppers can find freedom from our tendency toward selfish choices and rebelling against God's way by applying the blood Jesus shed to atone for our sins. And until the plague of sin is dealt with, no other efforts to rewire your identity matter. This plan to free our lives from the curse of our selfishness and rebellion is the gospel, or the good news, and it is the most important concept of this book. I'm not suggesting that receiving the Holy Ghost permanently cures all of your identity problems. You'll still need God to remind you of who you are. But not opening your heart to His Spirit *does* limit you in accepting an identity of power because of the plague of unremitted sin. Staying filled with the Holy Ghost and walking in the Spirit gives us right perspective on who we are, and it gets the curse of sin out of the way.

You have heard the old adage before, but it's still true: our identity is not in who we are but whose we are. I want to take that a step further: whose we are defines who we are. Our most important identity comes from first seeing ourselves as beloved children of God.

Life experiences, relational influences, and biological impulses that typically make up self-image are not the only factors for the Christian. The trump card must be the understanding of our identity as a born-again Apostolic. We are valuable because we are His—redeemed at an unthinkable price and filled with His Spirit: "But God, who is rich in mercy, because of His great love with which He loved us, even when we were dead in trespasses, made us alive together with Christ (by grace you have been saved), and raised us up together, and made us sit together in the heavenly places in Christ Jesus" (Ephesians 2:4–6). You can tell the value of something by how much you're willing to pay for it. Jesus was willing to pay the ultimate price to rescue us from the condemnation of our sin. We can't do anything to earn or buy His love, but when we accept what He has done for us, it changes our perspective of who we are. It even gives us a new lease on life if our past has marred our identity: "that you put on the new man which was created according to God, in true righteousness and holiness" (Ephesians 4:24). This notion of a new creature offers a special hope for identity formation. Lewis and Demarest claim, "The wisdom, moral uprightness, freedom of will, and fitness for eternity (the content of the *imago*), forfeited by sin, is restored to the believer in this life by the Gospel (1 Cor. 15:48; Eph. 4:21-24). . . . 'Grace brings about a historical transition from the old to the new man, to that man who is created after God's image in true righteousness and holiness.'"[1]

Redemption is the key to our hope: we can have a new identity! No matter who you are or were in the past, you do not have to be limited or labeled by that forever. When we are transformed by the work of the Holy Ghost, we are never the same. Our past is gone: "Therefore, if anyone is in Christ, he is a new creation; old things have passed away; behold, all things have become new" (II Corinthians 5:17). No other self-help program, psychological presentation, or cultural ceremony compares to this hope.

Unfortunately many Christians cannot grasp this reality. I meet so many young adults who are haunted by their pasts. We must realize our hope is not in a generic, fuzzy "God loves you" kind of greeting card message:

> But when the fullness of the time had come, God sent forth His Son, born of a woman, born under the law, to redeem those who were under the law, that we might receive the adoption as sons. And because you are sons, God has sent forth the Spirit of His Son into your hearts, crying out, "Abba, Father!" Therefore you are no longer a slave but a son, and if a son, then an heir of God through Christ (Galatians 4:4–7).

Because Jesus redeemed us with His own blood, we do not serve Him as though it were some work-for-hire arrangement. He bought us back or adopted us so we can fully embrace our rightful place as His child that He intended from the beginning of creation.

This biblical direction means, "Through the blood of Christ, our old identity never existed. It was destroyed upon the Cross and cannot be used to dominate or enslave us to who we used to be. . . . When we come to Him and relinquish ourselves, we receive a new identity. We are no longer who we once were; instead we are who He made us. We have a new purpose, direction, and outlook on life."[2] When old memories of past mistakes begin to replay in your mind, picture that moment as an online video clip and close the window. Visualize that screen with the video disappearing. Remind yourself of the new identity you have and the unlimited future God wants for you.

Pastor Glenn Murphy offers, "I have found that God can give you the grace and patience to deal with all of the embarrassing and humiliating circumstances in your life as well as the courage to make the necessary changes in your own mind. God can help give you the appropriate mindset and a perspective to see above it. You obviously can't change the horrible things that may have happened in your past, but you can change the way you think about them."[3] We cannot let our past trap us. If we have asked God to forgive us, then we must trust the power of His blood and expel the matter from our minds.

An Apostolic counselor said of shame: "It can be the result of all types of abuse, self-blame, self-hate, unresolved anger, false guilt, unforgiveness of self and others, allowing the past to define the self at present, etc. Salvation removed their sins but not their distorted God-concept of His truth. The fact of being a new creation in Christ has to be taught to the hurting person. A person can be transformed by renewing his/her mind with God's truth."[4] We must surrender our minds to God for complete transformation. When He forgives us, He removes the shame of our past.

The result of transformation should be that the Apostolic part of our identity is the noun and not the adjective in our identity. That sounds like grammar nerd talk, but humor me. Nouns are the subjects in a sentence. Adjectives are additional details that further describe those nouns. You are not a Pentecostal welder. You are a Pentecostal who welds. You're not an accountant who attends an Apostolic church. You are an Apostolic who is an accountant. Let me risk life and limb and take it one step further. You are not a mom who is Pentecostal. You are a Pentecostal who has children.

We don't have to wear any label we don't want to because we wear a name that is greater than any labels. When we are baptized in the name of Jesus, obeying the precedent of Scripture in Acts chapters 2, 8, 10, and 19, we receive new identity: "For as many of you as have been baptized into Christ have put on Christ" (Galatians 3:27, KJV). No other label matters; every other identity bows in subjection to the name of Jesus that becomes our identity in baptism. What an opportunity to start a new life:

> The unfathomable idea of an actual identity exchange is implicit in conversion. Jesus described the process in terms His hearers could understand. To Nicodemus He called it being "born again" or "born from above," indicating that spiritual life requires an identity change as drastic as a person's first entry to the world. As a result of this stuff-exchange, we carry within us not just the image of, or the philosophy of, or faith in, but the actual substance of God. One staggering consequence credits us with the spiritual genes of Christ: as we stand before God, we are judged on the basis of Christ's perfection, not our unworthiness.[5]

In addition to being made in the image of God, in salvation God's Spirit comes to dwell in us. When we receive the Holy Ghost and are baptized, our identity is transformed because we do not just carry the image of God but He Himself lives in us.

Brand Identity is an interesting concept to study. Rooted back in the days of cattle ranchers, the concept of a brand shows ownership in a tangible, clearly visible way. The marketing industry has picked up on the principle and incorporated it.

At the typical department store you can buy a purple t-shirt for around seven to twelve dollars. Add the official Louisiana State University logo to that same shirt and the price instantly triples.

It's amazing the difference a logo makes. It can be just the small letters of an organization's name and perhaps an icon or picture, but that name has a special meaning. It conveys a special identity that makes an ordinary item otherwise unnoticed suddenly special and of more value.

The American Marketing Association has not discovered a new concept with branding. God's people have always understood that His name is our identity and that He is the only one who provides a solution to our problems. We wear His name in baptism, which does both of these things: it marks us as belonging to Him and it is the only solution to our sin problem. And a life that might otherwise be ordinary, is suddenly different, of great value, and with access to great power because of an identity in Him.

We are peculiar in that we are purchased. We are branded, and we were never intended to hide from who we are. His people were never meant to look like everyone else, act like the unbeliever, or be confused with someone who's never taken on His name. Because we bear His name, we choose ourselves to be different in marks of devotion.

To the person who would feel worthless: His name and your identity in Him make you His prize.

To the person who would question your value to God: He loved you enough to give His life and His name to you—you are His beloved.

To the person struggling to understand the value of baptism: it offers the only solution to your problems by obliterating your past and giving you a new name and a new identity in Him.

To the person needing victory over your oppressors: you wear His name and with it you carry access to power to put your foot on the neck of your enemy.

The fix to this grasshopper effect of being trapped in insecurities and misplaced identity is not to stare in the mirror and repeat, "I will not be a grasshopper" six or eight times. The answer is to recognize you are a child of God, filled with His Spirit and bearing His name. In service to the King of kings and united with an army of fellow grasshoppers, your identity is not wrapped up in your personal statistics. When you understand and claim your Apostolic identity, nothing can stop you and God.

QUESTIONS FOR REFLECTION

- On a scale of 1 to 10, how often do you struggle with thoughts of frustration about who you are or things you have done in your past?
- Have you buried your old identity and the mistakes of your past by being baptized in the name of Jesus? Have you received the Holy Ghost so God lives in you? If not or if you're not sure, will you commit to a conversation with your pastor about God's plan for you as described in Acts 2, 8, 10, and 19?
- Have you ever let others influence your image of yourself? How can you redirect your priorities to make God your sole source of identity?

PRAYER

Almighty God, I recognize that You are God alone. And yet in all of your splendor and magnificence, You love me and saw me as valuable enough to give Yourself for me. Forgive me for times I have cheapened the price of Calvary by not believing I was worth saving. In this moment I accept that I am Your child and that Your love, Your gifts, and Your Spirit at work in my life give me my identity. Thank You for molding me in Your image. Help me today to understand all the ways You want to shape my identity so I can be the vessel You have created me to be.

CHAPTER 9

HOLY GRASSHOPPERS

love visiting my grandmother. I always have. It was a highlight
of my childhood and still remains one of the most special times
I have back home. Her mind is more than a steel trap; it's tita-
nium. She remembers intricate details of our family, and I love to
hear them.

One of the stories she tells is how Joel and I would play church
when we came to her house. A particularly memorable incident
happened when Joel was still too young to talk and I was just
a toddler. As the story goes, Joel and I sat on one couch in my
grandmother's living room and he pretended to drive the car as
we enacted the family trip to church. After an amount of time he
deemed suitable, we "arrived" and moved to the other couch in
the living room, which then became a church pew in our imagi-
nary world. We sang as I held a baby doll until without warning I
scowled at the doll and shoved it in Joel's direction. He dutifully
walked the doll down the hall to the church vestibule we presume,
and proceeded to firmly "redirect" the baby doll's attention for
church. Momentarily, he walked back to our "pew," handed me
the doll, and happily resumed church. That same night my dad
got a call from my grandmother. Why? Because as a long-time

educator, my grandmother knew that children reenact what they see their parents or caregivers live out, and apparently her little darlings were being "redirected" by someone.

Inherent in every child is a desire to be like his parent. As terrifying as that should be, it's a natural product of the way God made us. Infants are fascinated by their parents' faces. Toddlers learn to talk by mimicking the syllables Mom coos. Little ones tromp around in Dad's boots, imagining themselves to be a grown-up like Daddy.

In some sense this phenomenon paints the picture of how we should desire to be like our heavenly Father. Think back to the fact that God made man in His image. Sin and the Fall introduced corruption and broke that perfect communion with God. It could even be said that any good in humanity is just the residue of the image of God. However, with the atoning death of Jesus Christ, our spiritual adoption is made complete and we reclaim our rightful place as sons and daughters of God. Inherent in that process should be the birthing of a desire for communion with God. Because we seek to reflect the image of God, we should then study how we can be like Him.

Scripture points out some specifics:

- Jesus told us to be perfect [complete or whole] as our Father is perfect (Matthew 5:48).
- We are to be merciful just as our Father is merciful (Luke 6:36).
- We are to love as He loves (Ephesians 5:2).
- We are even to suffer as He suffered (I Peter 2:21).
- We are to walk in the light as He is in the light (I John 1:7).
- We are to walk [live] as He did (I John 2:6).

And so is it any wonder then that Scripture also declares, "but as He who called you is holy, you also be holy in

all your conduct, because it is written, 'Be holy, for I am holy'"
(I Peter 1:15–16). If reclaiming our God-given identity is about
living out our lives as children of God and reflecting His image,
then holiness is a natural outflow. Those original two humans
in the Garden lived in holiness before the introduction of sin.
We know that our final destination is a holy Heaven where sin
is forever banished. In this in-between stage you and I occupy
between the original Garden and the final Paradise, our commitment should be to pursue holiness amid a fallen world.

Let's start by defining holiness. Holiness is a topic so hotly
debated in such a range of religious circles it has become a pro-
verbial minefield—so much so that many ministers will not even
acknowledge it in their preaching, even though it is a biblical
principle and a signature tenet of Pentecostals. I don't presume
to provide an end-all, be-all explanation of holiness in one short
chapter. In fact, let me begin this chapter by referring everyone
to the pivotal work on holiness by David K. Bernard, *Pursuing Holiness*. What I can do, however, is suggest that holiness is living
in the image of God, conforming to His character, and separating
ourselves from sin unto God's purpose (Romans 12:1–2; II Corinthians 6:17–7:1).[1]

Building upon the progressive argument we've made in this
book, I propose that if we understand our lives to be a gift from
God, we take on His name in baptism, and we are filled with His
Spirit, He makes us holy. Putting holiness in this broader context,
we understand that "salvation begins with regeneration, or the
new birth; continues with sanctification, a process of progressive-
ly becoming more like Christ, and concludes with glorification, or
resurrection with an immortal body and sinless perfection. . . . We
do not produce our own holiness; we partake of God's holiness
(Heb. 12:10)."[2] If you've followed our argument that the grasshopper effect represents our resistance (for any number of reasons) to

embrace who God wants us to be, then you realize what an oxymoron "holy grasshoppers" is. How could we be holy without God and His work in our lives?

That question is a perfect starting point. To understand holiness, we must understand that God is holy. Since this book has established the value of being made in God's image and that because we are made in His image we should want to be like Him, it stands to reason we would seek to be holy. Peter understood this when he urged in I Peter 1:14–22 for Christians to rest in the grace that comes from God and reminded us of the message clear back from the Law given to Moses to be holy as God is holy.

You cannot separate God's love from His holiness, and part of God's love involves judging wickedness. When Isaiah saw God, it involved a revelation of His holiness and Isaiah's own insufficiencies (6:1–7). We serve a merciful God but He is also holy. Thankfully He invites us to be holy and makes us so (John 17:17).

We are His because He made us and we wear His name. But let's not forget we are His because He bought us with His blood; we are a purchased people. That same blood that washed away our sins at our initial conversion is the same blood that makes us holy each day (I Peter 1:19).

I am made holy by the blood of Jesus and not by any good thing I do. You've likely heard it, but it bears repeating: holiness is not list-keeping. Yet when we are made holy by His blood, we should want to live in a way that reflects that holiness. In that tension, parties emerge that champion grace and are labeled "loose with grace" and parties emerge that champion lifestyle and stewardship choices and are labeled "legalists." Isn't it a shame that we let one of the most precious gifts and responsibilities of our relationship with God become a battleground for theological debate? Without giving credence to further debate, I will simply say: holiness is about returning to who He called us to be—made in the likeness of His image. Since I am made in His image and He is holy, I simply choose to live in a way that reflects His image.

It would be impossible to write a book about who God made us to be without considering holiness as a component of Apostolic identity. The early Apostolics understood this well with Paul teaching extensively on holiness of heart, mind, and body. As I look around at a world where gender is being categorized as a social construct rather than a design of God, I can see in fresh ways I would have never imagined what a gift holiness is. In the beginning God created us male and female (Genesis 1:27). He intended our femininity or our masculinity to be a fundamental part of our identity. The way we treat our bodies and present our bodies should reflect that.

Holiness involves not just being separated from sin but being set apart for God's service.[3] Holy implements in the Old Testament were vessels that had been set apart and were no longer for common use. Thus while holiness begins with us being called out of sin and Jesus sanctifying us, He then commissions us and sends us back into the world to minister to others. We are made holy not just for our own benefit, but to serve Him. As Homer Ashby argues in *Our Home Is over Jordan: A Black Pastoral Theology*, we don't have to stay focused on what we came out of, but rather focus on what to do with our freedom.[4] We are not just sinners saved by grace; we are saints (holy people) of a living God with purpose. In response to the transforming work of Jesus in my life, I endeavor to go back into the world and minister to others. God has made me holy, so as I show His love and holiness to my world, people will be drawn to Him.

* * * * *

With New Orleans ranking as the third rainiest city in the US and three other cities in Louisiana making the top ten, the state's annual rainfall totals border on that of subtropical some years.[5] When we were kids in the early eighties, we had a year of particularly wet weather. Our parents bought us rubber boots from the revered TG&Y store in town. One day as my dad was working a horse in the riding pen between thunderstorms, he looked up to see four-year-old, rubber-boot-clad Joel running through the rain-filled ditch as fast as he could, kicking up water higher than his head.

Dad yanked the horse to a stop and called to Joel, "Joel, don't you get wet!"

Joel never slowed down and hollered back, "I'm trying not to!"

He had on rubber boots, after all. Wasn't the point of them so that you could do anything you wanted and were protected from the water?

My dad tells that story frequently and we chuckle at Joel's approach, but I wonder if Joel was onto something? His little boots were not made for sandy beaches or grassy hillsides. They were made for trekking through water holes and muddy bogs. Perhaps when God saved us from our sins and made us holy, He didn't intend for us to be put permanently in a trophy case. I'm not advocating we hang out in crackhouses every weekend with the false logic that holiness is a raincoat so we can put ourselves in spiritually corrupt and dangerous situations. That's not the point. What I am suggesting is that holiness was not a matter of God creating some hoops for us to jump through or an achievement test for us to take every week to feel good about checking a box. Holiness serves a purpose of reflecting the image of God to a hurting world.

While we proceed wisely, we must determine to show God's glory and holiness. Jesus' blood not only makes us holy, it becomes a beacon to others. After all, true holiness is a product of God's redeeming power at work in us. We need not cower at the thought of introducing holiness to our world. While we are to take sin seriously and not pride ourselves in a personal ability to be clean (since salvation and holiness come from God alone), we do not have to be held hostage by the threat of destruction from sin. J. Mark Jordan once said, "The love which God has for you provides a way to escape the insidious attacks of Satan, the frustrating weaknesses of your flesh and the propensity of the world to relentlessly fight against you. In spite of seemingly impossible situations, God has engineered a masterful plan to redeem you and give you everlasting life."[6] That same love and power in the shed blood of Jesus makes us holy. It works through us as a witness in a broken world to show others there is still a living Savior at work today.

The three Hebrew children would have to make the top five favorite stories in Sunday school class, and we will never outgrow the lesson learned. Logic dictates that when your life is threatened by the top dog, you do what you've got to do to live to fight another day. In a generation spared from the sacrifices of a war on the homefront, I speak as one unaccustomed to sacrifice in the name of God, family, and country. Our generation is a "just do it and pray about it later" group. In the new reality of forced tolerance, transgender civil rights, and churches being threatened legally to comply with same-sex marriage, the path of least resistance beckons temptingly.

Out of place are three Israelites who were so headstrong about their choice of worship and identity they put their lives on the line. You know the story: because they refused to bow and worship an idol god, they were thrown into what should have been a fatal fiery furnace. Miraculously, they were delivered by God. The lesson learned is that God protects and delivers those who stand for righteousness. However, for God to do the protecting part, the three captives had to do their part with the bow refusal. And that, my friends, took an identity check to end all identity checks. Note that the fiery furnace story was not some surprise event that caught the Hebrews off-guard. They had already charted an against-the-current course of dedication to holiness long before the showdown. Their refusal to take the path of least resistance, the inconvenient decision not to eat the king's meal plan, prepared them for the standoff.

With talk about being made in God's image and being loved infinitely by Him, we've got the ingredients needed to calculate a positive identity. Yet each of us must accept that identity as an individual in response to the call of Almighty God and make subsequent choices about how to pursue holiness in our lives.

Too often our temptation is to define something by what it is not. Little is the opposite of big. Cold is not hot. Normal is what I am and abnormal is anyone not like me. That last one is especially true. I don't do very well at understanding other people who aren't like me. For instance, why do companies make crunchy peanut butter? Clearly it is undesirable; surely no one would think of eating it. I know I won't. Normal is despising crunchy peanut butter.

Yet we can't define our identity by measuring ourselves against what we perceive to be normal. We must derive our identity and self-concept with different constructs—namely, the Word of God. The resulting choices of how we live our lives should reflect that unique identity.

We are called to be image bearers—to mirror God to our world. Since He is holy, we seek to mirror that holiness. That perspective directs the decisions of our daily life. Who you are—your core identity—is not established or destroyed by a handful of choices whether good or bad, but our perpetual lifestyle should be centered on a commitment to reflect His holiness. Who you are is determined by your identity as a child of the King. It is then up to you to live out that identity, which should be our compass in making godly choices that reflect our royal identity.

QUESTIONS FOR REFLECTION

- What did God redeem you from? Do you remember His goodness in your life?
- Are you using your redeemed life to point others toward God?
- In what areas of your life do you hear God calling you to greater consecration?

PRAYER

Jesus, thank You for Your blood that makes me holy. You know everything about me, every flaw and every carnal desire. I know that You have not redeemed me without purpose but that I am to point others back to Your mercy. I ask You to speak to me about areas of my life I can consecrate to be closer to You and to serve Your purpose more intently. I thank You for Your powerful blood that is always available to me so I am not cursed by sin. Father, guide me and use me to show others through Your holiness in my life that You are still at work today redeeming the captive.

CHAPTER 10

GRASSHOPPERS IN
NEED OF GRACE

The National Hurricane Center reports that North America endures an average of seven hurricanes every four years.[1] I grew up along the Gulf Coast and experienced my share of hurricanes—the empty shelves of grocery stores, the days without electricity and water, and the weeks of firewood cutting that follow—and remember not too fondly the devastation. As kids we were scared and as teenagers we were idiots looking for a reason to turn it into a party. Some things you don't outgrow, and one of the factors that always fascinates me are the people who won't leave. Just about every year, somewhere along the Gulf Coast, you'll hear the story about someone emergency officials beg to evacuate and offer unlimited resources to help, and yet these residents refuse, choosing instead to remain in the path of imminent danger.

Time magazine did an article in 2005 after Hurricane Katrina and branded this scenario as "Catastrophe Cowboy Syndrome: a cavalier attitude shared among so many on the Gulf Coast that they can stand up to, and ride out, threats like major hurricanes."[2] Sometimes fact is better than fiction, and the story of one catastrophe cowboy is wilder than anything I could make up.

On Saturday, August 27, 2005, Katrina took aim at New Orleans, and Mayor Ray Nagin called for a voluntary evacuation of the city where a man named Kevin Sloan lived. Like many other residents, Sloan refused to leave.

On Sunday, August 28, Katrina reached category 5 status with 160 mph winds, and Mayor Nagin ordered a mandatory evacuation of New Orleans. Sloan stubbornly remained in his home.

On Monday, August 29, Katrina made landfall, flooding the city (and Sloan's house) with snake- and debris-infested waters. Kevin Sloan climbed into the attic of his home as the waters rose, eventually broke a hole through the roof, and was one of the hundreds of people rescued by emergency workers.

You would think after such a harrowing ordeal that Kevin Sloan would be less prone to his catastrophe cowboy syndrome. But Sloan's story gets more interesting.

After his rescue, with his home flooded, Sloan hitchhiked the 156 miles from New Orleans to Abbeville, Louisiana, to stay with his uncle.

If you remember the summer of 2005, you know where this story is going.

September 18, less than three weeks after Katrina, Tropical Wave Rita formed near The Bahamas. Again evacuation orders were issued. Again emergency personnel offered to help southwest Louisiana flee the storm's deadly path. And you would think that of all people, Kevin Sloan would take up the offer of help and get out of harm's way.

But he did not.

On Saturday, September 24, floodwaters rose in the house where Kevin Sloan remained despite many offers of help to evacuate. Kevin Sloan once again found himself trapped in a home with flood waters rising.

There is a happy ending: someone came along in a boat and rescued Kevin. They took him to a helicopter, which carried him to a bus, which took him to a shelter in Lafayette where he was safe from the storm with hundreds of other rescued people—perhaps too stubborn, perhaps too proud to leave.[3]

I may be guilty of oversimplifying the issue, but I cannot help but think there is a certain degree of pride at work in this scenario. It seems from the outside looking in—from someone who now lives in the Midwest and is quick to trot to the basement when the tornado sirens go off—these cowboys think themselves invincible and will not recognize their need for help.

Yet while I can scratch my head at people like Kevin Sloan, even call them crazy and label their actions ridiculous, if I will be honest with myself, I have to admit maybe I see in myself some of that "cowboy" mentality when it comes to my spiritual life. Even after God saved me and made me holy, I still resort to managing my own spirituality.

Instead, the truth is everyone needs the mercy of God. I admire strength of character; I applaud people who have succeeded in life by hard work and determination. But when it comes to the state of our spiritual affairs, we need God's mercy.

In Luke 18:9–14 Jesus traveled to Jerusalem and encountered a group of people who "trusted in themselves that they were righteous, and despised others." Consequently Jesus told a parable that addresses the problem with trusting in ourselves and the self-assessment of our own righteousness. A Pharisee offered a lofty prayer of how good he'd been to God while a publican smote his heart in humility and asked God for mercy. An obvious reading of the parable is that God despises hypocrisy. We could talk about the dangers of comparing ourselves to others and passing judgment on those around us. That's certainly true, but there are also more complex layers at work in this text.

When we look at the Pharisee and go beyond the wrong spirit behind his prayer, we see a man who technically was doing the right things. If we just looked at the statistics, this man would make a pretty good saint: he was careful not to sin, he paid his tithes, and he went beyond the letter of the law with fasting twice a week. Statistically he would be considered a good Christian.

And yet those very statistics create his dilemma. If you look at his prayer, it actually reads as not a prayer so much as a reminder to God of how he has fared on his religious scorecard. Have you ever done that? "Hey, God, just making sure that you caught I worked in the nursery tonight? Did you see? That one kid puked on me twice. I think I oughta get bonus points."

Given the context of Jesus telling this parable in response to a group of people who had such "great confidence in their own righteousness," it's plausible to think this hypothetical Pharisee in the story represents the danger of thinking we can work our way into God's favor and mercy (Luke 18:9, NLT).

Now I doubt the last time you read the parable you identified with the Pharisee. My guess is you don't seek out a special seat of prominence during the worship service at your church, such as scholars believe the Pharisee in the parable would have done. I am confident you don't stage your offering at church in such a way as to make sure your gift is noticed, and I don't imagine you routinely thank God when you pray that you aren't a heathen like [fill-in-the-blank]. But is it possible we run the risk of falling into the same theological trap as the Pharisee? Though in theory his list of right acts and good living should have "earned" him God's favor, it did just the opposite. The worshiper who should've understood how to touch God failed to understand his enormous need of God's mercy and failed to even ask for it.

Instead a tax collector, typically known for corruption and extortion, walked away justified. In stark contrast to the worshiper who had all the boxes checked, this publican who self-identified as a sinner, discovered the depths of the mercy of God with just a seven-word prayer. The point? Even after salvation, we are still going to need God's grace.

His mercy is infinite—beyond what we can comprehend—and it's intrinsic in His nature to forgive us when we ask in humility and sincerity. One of the most hope-filled Scriptures in all of the Bible—our very lifeline—is I John 1:9: "If we confess our sins, he is faithful and just to forgive us our sins, and to cleanse us from all unrighteousness." If the promises of His Word are true, and we know that they are, we have the security of knowing when we need mercy, He is bound by His Word to extend it to us when we ask.

But that's the thing about mercy: we have to realize we need it. The most frightening part of the Pharisee and Publican parable is not just our human capacity for hypocrisy but our tendency toward crippling self-sufficiency.

In a Guinness Book of World Records kind of culture, we don't think we need mercy. In fact to be honest, we don't like mercy. Nobody wants to hear a story about a marathon runner who collapses from exhaustion and so the race officials have to pick him up in a motorized vehicle and drive him across the finish line. We want to hear about the guy who digs deep and edges across the finish line on a sprained ankle in record time by his own sheer grit. We don't want to hear about a business owner who couldn't make payroll but the government bailed her out; we want to hear the version of the story where she gets a second or third job and makes ends meet by burning the candle at both ends—a testimony to the power of hard work!

But though these poor analogies don't come close to portraying what God did for me, the truth is that His mercy did what my hardest work and best efforts could not do. I've been able to quote Titus 3:5 since I was a small child, but I don't know if I grasp what that really means. I don't know if I like mercy, because mercy means that I have to confess my own insufficiencies and surrender myself to God. Even when we recognize as grasshoppers that we are not as happy or strong or talented or [fill-in-the-blank] as others, our tendency is not to look for help but to find ways to sabotage those who bring our insufficiencies to the surface. The way it plays out with God is that during the moments I need to pray and find reconciliation with my Savior the most, I usually want to pray least. It's not fun facing who I am and how desperately I need Him.

A book made waves a few years ago, noted among other things for the honesty of the author in speaking of his need for grace. He claimed,

> I am too prideful to accept the grace of God. It isn't that I want to earn my own way to give something to God, it's that I want to earn my own way so I won't be charity.

> As I drove over the mountain that afternoon, realizing I was too proud to receive God's grace, I was humbled. Who am I to think myself above God's charity? And why would I forsake the riches of God's righteousness for the dung of my own ego. . . .

> Our "behavior" will not be changed long with self-discipline, but fall in love and a human will accomplish what he never thought possible. . . .

By accepting God's love for u
Him, and only then do we k
to obey.

In exchange for our humility and v.
accept the charity of God, we are given ∟
dom. And a beggar's kingdom is better than a
proud man's delusion.[4]

Like the author, we probably don't realize how mercy works. It would be so much more practical if God would just put price tags on things. You need a job? That's one thousand hours of prayer and ten days of fasting. You got carried away and told a little white lie? That'll be twenty hours of Bible reading and one sacrificial offering. Historically some religious groups have tried that and it has been problematic.

But while that's an extreme example, is it possible there is a thread of that thinking in the way we live? The last time you had a catastrophe, did you find yourself at any point bargaining with God—that you'd do anything if He'd just fix your problems? I do it every time I get a stomach virus. I've promised everything up to and including going on the mission field if the nausea will just stop.

It's hard for us to get our minds around mercy being free and God's love not being part of an exchange economy where we earn it or trade for it. Deep within us from the influence of our culture, authority structures, and in some instances our families, it is engrained that work and good behavior produce acceptance and benefits. I see more and more evidence around me that this thinking has prevailed upon the way we perceive God and His kingdom. We throw ourselves into Christian-y things without even realizing that quite often it's from a motive to gain God's love or acceptance. Without understanding His love is innate and can't be

, we work all the more furiously toward getting it. And when ave finally worn ourselves out trying to be good or we take a cation, all of our Christian living collapses because it was built on the wrong premise from the start. Think about it: if your version of Christianity is a routine of things to do and boxes to check to please God, at some point it's going to feel a lot like work. And the most diligent of workers get tired and have to have a break or paid-time off. Perhaps that's why some well-meaning Christians lapse in and out of faithful prayer, church attendance, or any number of things. With the wrong motivation, it's another job with a relentless pace. And overtime isn't very fun. And fun becomes the break away from work. And so Christian living by contrast is not fun. And you can see how the best intended commitments made at an altar can unravel.

We must have a recalibration of what motivates us. Paul told the Roman church it's sin that's work, and its wages cause fatalities (Romans 6:23). But God's eternal life is a gift. We are not in contract with God; we are not His employee or temp worker. We are His child, not conscripted to thankless tasks of prayer and service but gifted with the privilege to grow in closeness with Him and participate in expanding His kingdom. There is a fulfillment and peace that comes from resting in God's grace.

Understanding that He loves me and gives me sufficient grace motivates me to respond to that grace with sincerity—a balance between the fear (awestruck reverence) of the Lord and a peace in walking closely with Him. It's the irony of all ironies: I find my greatest strength when I humble myself before God; I find the vastest grace to live an overcoming life when I confess my depravity and recognize my salvation is entirely in God. I make no disclaimers nor add any asterisks: salvation comes only through the atoning death of Jesus Christ, not anything I can do to earn it. That revelation of a fundamental scriptural principle should free me from exhausting efforts to willpower my way into God's good graces. Our North American economic mindset and our self-sufficient culture clash with the idea of the King of all kings giving His life to extend mercy to us with no strings attached. But He did, and we need His mercy.

We've established that as fallen grasshoppers we continuously battle a selfish sin nature and any number of temptations. No theology of humanity is complete without establishing we are in need of grace. The good news is that when we're honest with ourselves, like David was in the face of incomprehensible sin, and we call on God, we have the hope of His Word that He will lovingly extend grace if we simply ask for it.

If we are willing to take God at His Word and accept His abundant grace, our lives should be changed as a result. First of all, we should be willing to change if God asks us to. The idea of changing may seem incongruous in a book about becoming confident in who God made you. But understand that our message of finding security in the identity God has given you is not a license to live brazenly blinded to your flaws. Our identity as a child of God made in His image comes from God and what He did. How you live out that identity is entirely another matter up to you.

While God makes us to be unique, we are not by default perfect. It stands to reason, then, that God in His mercy may call on us to make changes to be more closely conformed to His image. Paul advised, "Let him who stole steal no longer" because in His grace, God calls us into a new identity that sometimes requires change on our part (Ephesians 4:28). Though we've spent the better part of this chapter arguing grace is something God gives though we have done nothing on our part to earn it, the rest of the story is that in response we should seek to become more like the person God's Word calls us to be (II Timothy 3:17).

In addition to the Bible showing us how to make changes in our lives to better align with the identity God has graciously given, He will sometimes put people in our path to help us grow. If you are willing to listen to your pastor and men and women who love you, they can help you change and grow in areas where God is calling you to be more like Him.

Prayer and care is needed to navigate change in your life and even to decide if change is needed. You may encounter critical people for whom nothing you ever do is good enough. Again you must pray to determine which voices of love you will let speak into your life, knowing your identity-giver is Jesus, whose voice trumps all others. Yet that confidence is not a justification to overlook your flaws with a "that's just how God made me" shirk. Glenn Murphy instructs, "Are you willing to sacrifice who you are now for a new identity that will advance the Kingdom of God? Again, you may realize that what you need is not a personality change, but an acceptance of who God desires to make you into. Are you willing to try to improve yourself instead of hiding under an artificial image which you carry in public?"[5] If you are willing to grow as God directs, He will give you the grace to do so, and you will be the better for it.

Finally, as a result of God's grace in our lives, we should be willing to extend grace to others. I'll illustrate my case with another proof, thanks to a compelling geometry teacher in ninth grade.

Given: God freely gives grace to all (Ephesians 4:7).
Prove: I should show grace to others.

Statement	Reason
1. God extends grace to me.	I John 1:9
2. I am called to bear God's image and represent Him to others.	Ephesians 5:1; I Peter 2:21
3. I should show grace to others.	Luke 6:36

This is a hard pill to swallow for the self-appointed baroness of the fairness brigade; I take that responsibility very seriously. In my book we only should have to be nice (and patient) to the people who deserve it. Grace throws a monkey wrench in my philosophy because by its very definition it is undeserved. Yet if I am to be like Him and if I am to bear His image so the whole world can see Him, it means making the godly choice to be gracious when a swift kick to the face feels more in order. Think of the witness. Could there be anything more miraculous than being merciful when road rage feels perfectly legitimate?

I do not intend to make light of the fact that mercy is difficult. This chapter does not presume to speak of issues of abuse or offer direction in legal and personal safety matters. A number of disclaimers are probably in order, and I am not arguing that a Christian should be a doormat without common sense. Can I step back and simply offer the challenge that generally speaking we as Christians should reflect the love of God? Paul included among his final instructions to the church at Philippi, "Let your gentleness be known to all men" (Philippians 4:5). Is it too much to suggest that a child of God filled with His Spirit should be marked by the fruit of the Spirit, which include love, joy, peace, longsuffering, gentleness, goodness, faith, meekness, and temperance (Galatians 5:22–23). As a result of God's grace, we should mirror God's grace to others (Ephesians 4:32).

QUESTIONS FOR REFLECTION

- Can you identify with the Pharisee in the parable? Perhaps you're doing all the right things, but could it be that God sees something in your heart you haven't bothered to ask Him to reveal? Are you willing to ask God to show you what's inside your heart?
- Have you found yourself exhausted in efforts to earn God's love? Why?
- How can you pursue a deeper relationship with God that continuously grows in His grace?
- Is there someone to whom you need to show grace the way God has extended it to you?

PRAYER

Jesus, You have been merciful to me. I know that. But sometimes I don't talk to You about everything that is in my heart. I do a lot of good things, and it's easy from the way the world and the people around me trade good behavior for favors to forget You look at more than just the things I do. I know You look at my heart, and I know that I need Your grace. I recognize I am not righteous on my own. I need Your grace. I ask You today to have mercy on me and to forgive my sins. I pray that You would help me keep a humble Spirit and to always recognize my need for Your mercy. Thank you for the promise of Your Word that there are no qualifications for mercy or strings attached. I rejoice in the hope that You will grant me grace when I ask.

CHAPTER 11

GIFTED GRASSHOPPERS

When I was in college I got a good deal on a '98 Camaro in the parking lot of our town's barber shop. I suppose you have to own a sports car at least once in your life; I just happened to get it out of the way early. Skittles, as we would christen it, was a stick shift with dual exhausts and a classic straight six. I still have no idea what those last three words mean, but it was a big deal to my dad. Every time I cranked Skittles, the whole car trembled like a quarter horse about to explode from a starting gate, and the pipes roared like a Harley. It was slightly terrifying, but I eventually got used to it.

I knew having a Camaro was supposed to be cool, but I had no idea what to do with Skittles. My driving consisted of commuting back and forth to school and the invariable Chili's run after church on Sunday nights. Skittles could have been a Toyota Echo and I'd not have known the difference.

But all of that changed one night. Tuesdays were my long day because I had a night class—Seventeenth-Century Literature from 6:00 to 9:00 PM, a real barn-burner. That particular evening I left the class and started the twenty-four-mile commute home, only to hit a traffic jam on I-12. After alternating between inching forward and sitting still for what felt like hours, I finally got to an off-ramp. I'd seen my dad use the exit to cut through the gravel roads of old hunting clubs in the parish and get home, and so I took off, eager to make up time.

I really don't know how fast I was going, but the phrase "too fast" substitutes aptly for lack of an exact speed. A ninety-degree left turn jumped out at me, and I realized too late I couldn't take it. Maybe on a surface other than gravel the outcome would have been different. As it was, things got hairy very quickly. It was as though there was so much action churning up front in the car, the back end couldn't keep up. Fishtailing quickly gave way to all-out Tilt-a-Whirl-style revolutions. Skittles spun around several times in the middle of the road and finally slid to a stop in the dried up ditchbank. It scared me pretty good to be sure, but I also remember at the same time being a bit in awe at the sheer power of that motor—whatever its specs. Instantly I knew in all my simple commuting I had never scratched the surface of the capability that rested beneath the hood.

I can't help but wonder if we've treated God's gifts in our lives the same way at times? Do we realize the degree of power and the extent of talents God has entrusted to us?

We know from Genesis that God gave humanity authority. Think about it. The original grasshoppers were gifted with authority for a purpose: to dress and keep the Garden and be in communion with God. They lost sight of that purpose and privilege, trading it for the false promise of secret knowledge and power.

Fast-forward to the children of Israel. God had gifted them with leaders who could be trusted and who had spiritual authority, as they'd seen firsthand through the plagues in Egypt and the parting of the Red Sea. God was also very specific in directing them with the purpose of possessing a promised land. Again, we see God's people trading the good things of God because of listening to wrong voices, failing to see themselves for who they were, and giving in to a counterfeit version of reality.

Fast-forward yet again to Jesus and His inner circle of disciples. He gifted them with His mentorship, revealing truths about the Kingdom, and teaching them to operate and minister in the spiritual realm. Still, one of those disciples would be blind to the reality of the privilege he had as being one of Jesus' twelve chosen disciples and would trade in that identity for his own version of a better deal. Little did he know, the results would be fatal.

Perhaps in light of Judas's tragic decision, Jesus would explain to the Twelve in their final moment of the Last Supper, "You did not choose Me, but I chose you and appointed you that you should go and bear fruit, and that your fruit should remain, that whatever you ask the Father in My name He may give you" (John 15:16). The disciples had a specific identity as Jesus' chosen, select vessels; the purpose of going out and bringing forth fruit in the form of establishing new believers; and the promise of authority.

Jesus is still looking for followers who will join this special mission today. Just as Jesus then gave authority and identity for a purpose, He gifts us today with talents and power to continue to establish His kingdom. He promised signs would follow believers—the only prerequisite was belief, and we still believe today (Mark 16:17–18). If, then, we accept these verses as still applicable, our inheritance includes signs and wonders. For those who will embrace their identity as His children, He equips with weapons that are "mighty in God for pulling down strongholds" (II Corinthians 10:4).

Specifically, Paul taught on the spiritual gifts God endowed to the church (I Corinthians 12). You know the text; it promises gifts of healing, miracles, prophecy, discernment, and more. This is not the picture of a handful of intimidated grasshoppers overwhelmed by their environment. No, the image is one of a triumphant army that cannot be stopped (Matthew 16:18).

This authority and these spiritual gifts, however, are not the only ways God blesses us to fulfill His purpose. In handcrafting us, He also gave us individual talents to use for the purpose of building His kingdom.

This concept is not without precedent. Remember Bezaleel? God told Moses He was giving Bezaleel the artistic talents needed to create much of the Tabernacle (Exodus 31:1–4). Yet if this were a lottery where God discriminately dropped on every 13,784th person some creative talent, it's hard to leverage that into motivation to believe my identity is special. But our story doesn't stop there.

God went on to tell Moses, "I have put wisdom in the hearts of all the gifted artisans, that they may make all that I have commanded you"—God gifted an army of people (Exodus 31:6). God gifts us all for service in His kingdom. This language isn't a fluffy mantra with no scriptural basis: "Each one has his own gift from God, one in this manner and another in that" (I Corinthians 7:7). We have a promise that God gives special abilities to each of us.

A study of the topic would be disingenuous if it did not include the parable of the Talents in Matthew 25:14–30. Our frequent contemporary conversations about stewardship would almost suggest the piggy bank hugger in the story should be the hero. Instead, the master was angry with him. I struggled with that story as a child. Wasn't the guy just trying to be careful to not get in trouble, and in the end that was exactly what happened anyway? The parable makes sense when I kick out my North American concept of money and think of the talent as a personal gift or ability. Substitute a carpenter who watches his church struggle with a building project and refuses to volunteer help. That scenario changes the story. Perhaps withholding my abilities from God's kingdom angers God.

I would be remiss if I did not also bring up the parable of the Prodigal Son. We frequently use the narrative to understand the process and psychology involved with those leaving the church and a portrait of how Jesus watches for the lost and how the church should behave likewise. While certainly those applications are valid, the original meaning of the word "prodigal" indicates to waste a resource. Part of the Prodigal's demise was that he wasted his opportunities and gifts. While those gifts were primarily material resources in the story, the principle holds true for the spiritual gifts and individual talents God endows to us. When we misuse or run from those gifts, we are rejecting our identity as His son or daughter—making a selfish or insecure choice to leave the good gifts from God to create our own (lesser) things we think we want. The Prodigal was determined to be on his own, rejecting the roles, provisions, and gifts that were inherent as the son of a loving, generous father. We can tsk-tsk at the Prodigal and easily see the imprudence of his pigpen-destined decision, and yet how much more wasteful is it for us to reject or fail to recognize the gifts our Creator and Father extends to us as His sons and daughters.

If we really want to be His royal heirs and not headstrong grasshoppers who resist the identity given by Him, we should look for the gifts He has placed in our lives and commit ourselves to using them for His purpose. When we use our talents for God's purpose, we fulfill His will and plan for our lives. And the best way to realign your identity with God's perspective is to go to work fulfilling His purpose.

QUESTIONS FOR REFLECTION

- Without excuses or apology, describe the gifts you believe God has placed in your life.
- Are you using your gifts in ways that honor God?
- How can you further dedicate your talents to God's service?

PRAYER

Father, You are gracious in ways I'll never deserve. You have shown favor and blessed me with gifts. Forgive me for times I have taken my talents for granted or failed to use them in ways that honor You. I recognize that every good gift in my life is a blessing from You that you have trusted me to steward. Jesus, please help me to use my talents for the service of Your kingdom. I ask today for direction in how I can develop and dedicate all the gifts You have put in my life back to You. I will give my talents for Your service without excuse or apology. Thank You for Your favor and blessings in my life.

CHAPTER 12

GOLIATH-SIZED GRASSHOPPERS

What a picture of confidence. Think about it. This guy had no hang-ups. And why should he? He was nine feet tall for crying out loud. He towered over the masses. He had never met anyone who intimidated him.

And that was his problem. He had no perspective of himself. He was submitted to no one. The result was an arrogance that was abhorrent to God. Goliath hurled not only challenges but blasphemies at God's people. And what did God do? He sent the most unlikely of candidates to defeat the all-confident monster.

Yes, David's story is encouraging and should remind us we're not defeated grasshoppers, even against giants, even when those around us try to tell us so. But the other character in the story presents a lesson as well.

Goliath
- Veteran warrior
- 9' tall
- 126 pounds of armor
- A spear the size of a fence rail
- A bully who had verbally abused the Israelite army for over a month
- Absolutely zero inhibitions, fear, or self-doubt

Goliath represents self-confidence run amuck. He also represents a monumental revelation for us. While most of us tend more often to be Gideons than Goliaths, there is the danger of becoming a Goliath. If the enemy can't get us on our insecurities, he'd love nothing more than to tempt us with the other extreme—convince us of all our value that no one else can approach, twist our gifts in our mind, convince us we're superior to all others, and create a monster of arrogance. Such thinking runs counter to everything we've established about being made in God's image. No, we're not helpless, but we're also not invincible. We're flawed human vessels God graciously chooses to redeem, heal, and use.

So how do we avoid arrogance? We understand that the Bible speaks clearly about the danger of pride—that abominable display of carnality that comes from unchecked submission to a divinely ordered hierarchy of God and others first. We've simply got to work on something not so simple: humility.

Dr. Everett Worthington, psychologist and author of a recent book on humility through the perspective of Christian psychology, analyzed several scientific experiments and studies and determined that humility is impossible to measure. It can't be self-assessed because of the paradox of the nature of humility and modesty, and it can't accurately be calculated by others:

"Humility shows up as modesty without a hint of false modesty. It involves an absence of arrogance, pride, and narcissistic entitlement. It incorporates honesty with self and sensitive honesty with others (not presuming to tell others unwanted or unhelpful—though honest—feedback). But mostly humility shows up as unselfish service on behalf of others."[1] Easy enough, right?

Let's revisit the spies in Numbers 13. We've established that their issue was a matter of wrong perspective—refusing to recognize their identity as God's children. By the same token, Goliath didn't see himself correctly as the grasshopper he was in comparison to Almighty God. Goliaths really are grasshoppers who are simply blinded to reality. Unfortunately that's what pride does; it is a parasite that blinds its host to the reality of limitations.

In contrast to Goliath, let's look at David.

David
- Youngest child
- Previously overlooked for consideration as a candidate for the throne
- Shepherd and errand runner
- Combat experience limited to lion and bear
- Unable to properly use standard military-issue weaponry

You know the rest of the story: God used unlikely David to defeat the brawny heathen Goliath. And David knew enough to understand it was God who was the hero of the story.

So what exactly was it about David that was special—so special we use him as the ultimate underdog story even outside religious circles? Certainly the favor of God rested upon him and God specially guided that smooth stone on a missile mission to the giant's forehead. But couldn't God have done that with any other Israelite warrior? There must have been some quality in David that positioned him to be chosen by God.

First we have to recognize his faithfulness to his small charge as a young shepherd. God seems to notice those who take their purpose and responsibility seriously (Luke 16:10). Next, there was that Joshua factor in David—something within him that reared its head when Goliath dared to defy God and His people: "who is this uncircumcised Philistine, that he should defy the armies of the living God?" (I Samuel 17:26). Finally, David threw off the armor, choosing to leave his weapons in God's hands and notably declaring:

> You come to me with a sword, with a spear, and with a javelin. But I come to you in the name of the LORD of hosts, the God of the armies of Israel, whom you have defied. This day the LORD will deliver you into my hand, and I will strike you and take your head from you. And this day I will give the carcasses of the camp of the Philistines to the birds of the air and the wild beasts of the earth, that all the earth may know that there is a God in Israel. Then all this assembly shall know that the LORD does not save with sword and spear; for the battle is the LORD's, and He will give you into our hands (I Samuel 17:45–47).

David understood something every believer must claw out and etch into the brain: any abilities we have come from God and are His for the taking. This revelation and lifelong understanding was what could guide David to patiently trust God through years of living in caves and running for his life when he had every reason to expect a king's robe and the power of the throne. Humility is about more than not boasting; true humility is a life condition that involves recognizing God is the source of everything of merit in our lives and ceding all control to Him.

This brand of humility understands where true strength comes from. It doesn't mistake dependence on God for weakness. Though writing about the necessity of humility for leaders, N. Graham Standish's advice rings true for all Christians:

> [Humility] means bringing an attitude, a disposition of radical openness to God. . . . It means to be strong in seeking God's way and then to have the courage to lead others in God's direction despite the resistance and outright opposition by those who want us to follow the ways of the culture and of convention. It exposes us to our own weakness, powerlessness, fear, and anxiety. The way of humility invites us to follow God's path . . . that emphasizes meekness and weakness, leaving us open to the manipulations of those devoted to wielding power. If we are to become humble leaders, we have to develop a different kind of strength. This strength is a strength of character that few are willing to form, a strength of the Spirit that has its roots in Christ's way rather than the world's way.[2]

It would be an easy way out to draw up a list of don'ts as the trail to humility—don't wear this brand, don't drive this kind of car, don't say things like [fill in the blank]. That's not the measure of humility. What if instead of don'ts we focused on do's: do seek God's direction, do follow His whisper—understanding fundamentally that submission to God is the key to genuine humility.

William Temple, former archbishop of Canterbury, is quoted as having said, "Humility does not mean thinking less of yourself than of other people, nor does it mean having a low opinion of your own gifts. It means freedom from thinking about yourself at all."[3] We don't usually think of selflessness as freedom, but think of it for a moment. What if you never worried again about if people thought you looked good or if your clothes were stylish or if you were funny or smart? Imagine the liberty in not obsessing about yourself but merely going through life without a second thought about those things. That is the gift of selflessness.

In contrast, researchers tell us, "Arrogance is about fear: fear of personal inadequacies, fear that people will find out the 'truth.'"[4] What a pity to be bound by that kind of fear when we were hand-crafted by a God who does all things well. It is this understanding of who we are as God's children that gives us our humility.

Arrogance is the Pharisee whose only prayer is to thank God he's not like the publican (Luke 18:9–14). It's the disciples having a petty debate over who could sit where in Heaven (Matthew 18:1–4). If you remember, Jesus' answer in those scenarios was to say forgiveness was granted to the humble publican and to advise His followers become like children.

In a letter whose context is to compliment a church effectively living out the Christian faith, Paul nevertheless reminded the star pupils,

> Let nothing be done through strife or vainglory; but in lowliness of mind let each esteem other better than themselves. Look not every man on his own things, but every man also on the things of others. Let this mind be in you, which was also in Christ Jesus: Who, being in the form of God, thought it not robbery to be equal with God: But made himself of no reputation, and took upon him the form of a servant, and was made in the

likeness of men: And being found in fashion as a man, he humbled himself, and became obedient unto death, even the death of the cross (Philippians 2:3–8, KJV).

Ouch. Even the front row Christians were reminded that we can't keep score and we have to be thoughtful of others. What's more, Paul pulled the God card. He said if we really want to follow God, we have to follow in the footsteps of ultimate humility: putting others so far ahead of self we're willing to die for them. That concept grates against our innate selfishness and yet if are we trying to connect back to the image of God, it's a necessity.

In a seminal work establishing that the earliest Christians understood Jesus to be the fleshly manifestation of God, scholar Richard Bauckham makes a thought-provoking statement about the identity of God: "Since the exalted Christ is first the humiliated Christ, since indeed it is *because* of his self-abnegation that he is exalted, his humiliation belongs to the identity of God as truly as his exaltation does. The identity of God—who God is—is revealed as much in self-abasement and service as it is in exaltation and rule."[5] It takes a second to wrap your mind around it, but digging through Bauckham's argument brings a glimpse of God we wouldn't normally consider. Because of God's great love for us, He was as willing to condescend and be flesh to die to save us as He was to create the planets and rule the many people groups of history. That says something about who God is. And if we are to be like Him and attempt to live out our identity in His image, we must have a humility that is based in a willingness to put others first and be servants.

Perhaps the greatest Christians are those who have learned to turn their focus from self to God and others. If we could really do that, perhaps our world would not be plagued by the pratfalls of narcissism, insecurity, and pride.

We need a good wake-up call to realize our frailty. While not a license to avoid attempts to be our best, I think confronting our weaknesses is an honest reminder that we will fail at times despite our best efforts; we must realize that in advance and work on how we will handle these failures. That doesn't quite have the ring to it you might expect of a book on identity, but I think it's healthy to be very honest with ourselves and recognize our weaknesses. This in turn brings us back to the feet of God—the only place we can find the grace and direction to live in humility despite our weaknesses, flaws, and failures.

Perhaps being transparent is not so much about admitting sordid details of personal failures as it is openly confessing a thorough need for the grace and strength of God. In Jacob's case, the limp was not so much a weakness as the visible sign of time in God's presence. Maybe as Christians we don't necessarily need to broadcast details of our own weaknesses so much as show by our character that we have spent time in God's presence. I'm challenged to ask myself, "Besides what I say, do my actions show a limp—dependence on and proof that I've been with Him?"

What would my neighbors think if I could really live like this? Sometimes I'm afraid to wonder how I'm doing in reflecting the image of God, particularly when it involves these heart issues. One author challenged, "Gracious, self-forgetful humility should be one of the primary things that distinguishes Christian believers from the many other types of moral, decent people in the world. But I think it is fair to say that humility, which is a key differentiating mark of the Christian, is largely missing in the church. Nonbelievers, detecting the stench of sanctimony, turn away."[6] God help us.

As dangerous as it can be to look for formulas for Christian living, a starting place for humility is to love what you serve more than you love yourself. Humility means sacrificing oneself for the good of something grander and nobler—a feat all but lost in today's egocentric culture. As Christians we would do well to be reminded of the need for becoming lost to self and pretense and finding our identity within the mission of God's kingdom, of all things grandest and most noble.

As bearers of the image of God, we need look no further than Calvary for history's ultimate act of humility. The King of kings "made Himself of no reputation, taking the form of a bondservant, and coming in the likeness of men. And being found in appearance as a man, He humbled Himself and became obedient to the point of death, even the death of the cross" (Philippians 2:7–8). William Booth Clibborn said of the Incarnation it was a condescension that God "laid aside His splendor, stooping to woo, to win, to save my soul."[7] Never was humility more on display than when the holy God of Heaven, Creator of all things, became flesh, came to earth in a meager stable, and gave Himself up to be mocked and tortured—all so you and I could come to an altar and receive His mercy. When I truly see Calvary and come face to face with what happened there, my perspective on humility is realigned. Living near Calvary is critical to maintaining a humble spirit.

Humility formation is difficult since experts have stated repeatedly that it cannot be learned but only acquired through hard-knock life experiences. Yet if we commit to maintaining an intimate, consistent relationship with God, we position ourselves correctly. True Christian humility is the realization that everything we are comes from God. Anything good within us is what He has placed there. Any achievements are not due to our talent or brilliance but the working of the Spirit and His gifts.

> **Take-aways:**
> • Recognize our feeble limitations without God's help
> • Maintain submission to God and leaders
> • Use our talents for the good of God's kingdom

A few years ago I decided to take up golf because some friends were into it. Golf is a sick and demented game. You'll spend four hours hunting an egg-sized ball through woods and digging it out of creeks and ponds and vowing you'll never waste this much time again all to hit a single solid shot and be hooked anew. It sucks you in and you're never the same. True to my competitive nature, I became determined to get to the point I could play a round without embarrassing the family.

So I began taking classes through our local community college. In the second class the instructor silently watched me swing for several minutes and then offered this assessment: "You're on the verge of being a decent golfer." (I didn't know if I wanted to high-five him or hook him with my five iron.) While I tried to dissect his appraisal he continued, "What you have to do is instead of focusing on trying to make a good shot, you need to focus on not making a bad shot."

I have to tell you I was disappointed with that advice. Who wants to spend a golf round (or life, for that matter) just trying not to goof it up swing by swing? This humility thing is tricky business. Maybe we don't write books or preach sermons on humility because it just seems like a matter of not saying or not doing prideful things. We could ask ourselves what an arrogant person does and says and just try not to do that. However, there has to be more to humility than just the absence of blatant arrogance.

What if true humility is not about actions or words but a deeper heart condition? What if humility is decided by the way we think about God and consequently about ourselves?

We hope this book challenges you to recognize your value as loved and created by God with inestimable worth. But that recognition must be rooted in gratitude to God without arrogance about your gifts. A proper perspective of who we are as a vessel of God displaces pride. It's hard to take pride in a rented tuxedo. We have been blessed with bodies, minds, and talents that are good, but they are on loan from God. As simple as it is, the answer to maintaining the humble, contrite heart God loves is remembering everything good about us is from Him.

QUESTIONS FOR REFLECTION

- Certainly there are areas of our lives for which we can be thankful and take confidence. What are those areas in your life?
- How do you guard against arrogance concerning those gifts?
- Do you have someone in your life who will call you on it if you lose a paradigm of humility? If so, take time today to remind that person of how much you need him or her to be a voice of caution in your life. If you have never had a conversation like that, think of someone you could trust to help you be accountable for maintaining a right spirit.

PRAYER

Father, if I say right now that I am humble, I have fallen into that circular trap of then not being humble. I want to have a right heart and a right spirit. I need Your help in this pursuit every day. So Jesus, I ask You to help me keep a right focus and remember that every good thing in my life is a result of Your grace. Today I say thank You for those unfailing mercies.

CHAPTER 13

GRASSHOPPERS AT WORK

There's nothing particularly glorious or romantic about the work I do each day righting comma splices and rearranging print schedules. Joel, on the other hand, has lived out the great American adventure as a professional cowboy. He trained a number of horses for clients and worked for three A-lister horse trainers before changing careers. With the thousands of horses he's ridden, I'm most intrigued by a recent case of his.

My father raised a striking bay mare a few years ago. She was from prize stock—a pedigree long and prestigious with performance details I won't recount. We had high hopes for this filly; she was as athletic as she was eye-catching. Western-style riding depends on the smoothness of gait, and this mare showed great promise. So after investing nearly two years of the best feed and care, my Dad sent the filly to Joel to be trained. From looks to pedigree to the environment of her upbringing to her natural abilities—all signs pointed to a champion.

And so we were disappointed when Joel began sharing concerned progress reports as the months passed. In the western class, the horse is supposed to slowly drive her hind legs forward and smoothly swing her front legs into place, all in a way that communicates effortless grace. This mare had naturally flat front-knee action, a coveted quality. But as Joel pushed her to drive those hind legs, she struggled. Physically she had the talent, but when pushed she tried so hard to do what the rider asked, she would become a basket case. Overeager to please, she would hop in place, exaggerating the hind leg action Joel cued, losing her forward momentum, and getting frazzled—the ultimate self-destructive overachiever in horse form.

Recently we were all home together again, and I watched Joel ride the mare. He pushed her to improve her footwork, and before long she was right back in that destructive pattern—tail swishing (a sign of anxiety) and chewing the bit in frustration—like a kid in near panic trying to keep up with a faster-moving adult.

The reality of North American life is that work forms a vital part of who we are. As such, our Christianity must include an approach to work. Even half a century ago theologians understood this truth: "We recognize and understand that to live is to labor, so that one searching and realistic description of man is *Homo faber*, Man the worker. It is, then, abundantly clear that unless our religion can address itself to our work with powerful and illuminating insights, our religion will be out of touch with a large and important part of our life and will be hard put to escape the damaging charge of irrelevancy."[1] Certainly our theology should acknowledge the value of and need for work. Yet is it possible we have let our careers consume us? Have we become the talented bay mare so obsessed with being successful at our work that we let it consume and derail us? Statistics say that Americans take less vacation and work longer hours than their counterparts in other countries.[2] Have we let work become our god instead of letting work be a reflection of our relationship with the true God?

On the other hand, some good-hearted, well-meaning Christians hate their jobs. Take this recent sentiment: "Work is something we do, and often endure, simply to keep life and limb together. Most of us put up with the difficult realities of our daily work because we have to."[3] How sad to think many have no hope of finding meaning in their work or even moderate enjoyment. There is a danger of overlooking this topic in the church as Gary Erickson explains, "Due to a lack of preaching and teaching about work, I believe that many church members are being robbed of one of the great joys of the Christian life—the spiritual satisfaction of fulfilling personal callings, giftings, and careers. I believe that many church members do not achieve their full potential because of an ambivalent view of their daily work. They fail to understand that their daily work is weaved monolithically with their spiritual lives."[4] In the face of such a spectrum of viewpoints on work, let's attempt to recalibrate our theology of work.

God reveals Himself in Scripture first as a God who is at work creating the worlds. As God's image bearers, we reflect who He is in every way, including a proclivity to work. Erickson elaborates, "From the beginning God made man and woman for work. This job description comes from a God who is himself a worker. As creatures created in God's image, human beings are workers as well."[5] As Apostolics loyal to Scripture, we can't overlook this earliest biblical injunction to work: God put Adam and Eve in the Garden and gave them a job to do in dressing and keeping it. The New Testament goes on to establish the value of work. It serves the function of providing for our families, and the Bible is very clear about that responsibility (I Timothy 5:8; II Thessalonians 3:12).

While work does have a pragmatic function of meeting our basic material needs, we must consider if our work has spiritual value. "For some, work is only the means to make money to pay our bills. Work, for them, is at the bottom of the eternal temporal hierarchy."[6] Could we be missing something with this view? For a God who knows the number of hairs on our head, why do we suppose He wouldn't care about what we do with one-third of our waking lives? Erickson cites R. Paul Stevens, who believes your career can be a call from God, and argues, "There is a divine propensity toward work which dignifies all work that is a response to a divine 'calling.'"[7] We do and should have Apostolics who are called to be mechanics, accountants, teachers, surgeons, florists, marketing creatives, and so much more. If we make our career—like every other area of life—a matter of prayer, submitted to the will of the Master, we can expect Him to direct us and call us into vocations for His purpose and glory.

It's not just a cute idea to think God would take interest in our work; it's the only God-centered option out of the array of philosophical and theological explanations:

> Without any theology of vocation we lapse into debilitating alternatives: fatalism (doing what is required by the "forces" and the "powers"); luck (which denies purposefulness in life and reduces our life to a bundle of accidents); karma (which ties performance to future rewards); nihilism (which denies that there is any good end to which the travail of history might lead); and, the most common alternative today, self-actualization (in which we invent the meaning and purpose of our lives, making us magicians). In contrast the biblical doctrine of vocation proposes that the whole of our lives finds meaning in relation to the sweet summons of a good God.[8]

No, we must believe work—like every other area of our lives—must be surrendered to God and used for His purpose and glory.

Of course like anything else, a good gift can be misused. Solomon found no purpose in work (Ecclesiastes 2:4–11). He watched people toil and labor to pile up toys and still live empty lives. However, he shows us not that work is vain but that the motives of our heart dictate how work can be misused. Idleman sounds a contemporary warning: "Work and achievements are blessed by God, and have been since Adam and Eve received their work assignments in the garden. But they are ways of feeling the joy of serving God. Once they become something else, they can be toxic."[9] Instead we must focus on this idea of "the joy of serving God" and understand work as an opportunity to honor our Creator (I Corinthians 10:31). We were called to reflect His glory even, and especially, in work.

LET'S ASK THE TOUGH QUESTIONS NOW:

Q: What is the balance between our weekly job and our work at church? How do we reconcile the conflict we feel over giving away forty hours of our life to a secular job and where does ministry fit in?

A: God can direct you to a vocation and use it as a testimony to show His glory. That does not have to operate in competition with the biblical injunction to seek first the kingdom of God (Mark 6:33). If we look at every area of our lives as a way to serve God's kingdom and prayerfully seek His direction, God will guide us in decisions about how to balance and prioritize our lives. As we seek God and look for opportunities to serve Him and bring Him glory, He will open doors for our day-to-day work and in service in His Kingdom. God blesses us with godly pastors who can direct us in how to serve God in our local church.

Q: We know that a works-based mentality toward God is a bad thing. If we should work as a way to give glory to God, how is this not turning into a works-oriented approach to Christian living?

A: Work can and should be an offering of worship to God, and yet our motive behind that work has to be in check. We don't work to make God love us; we work because He loves us. We are not human doings. Phrases like "doing life" should be red flags. Life is meant to be lived out as a journey and an experience. It isn't something we "do" the same way we do the laundry or check off items on a grocery run. We are not machines and life is not a task to accomplish.

That thinking pervades our culture and creates a performance addiction that can consume us like our overachieving bay mare that self-destructed because she put too much pressure on herself to perform. We must rewire any motives that are based on the fallacy that God loves us because of what we can do. We can't project onto Him the kind of conditional, performance-based love we sometimes feel from those around us. He loves you. The end. Separate your motive to work from your faith that He loves you. Then after grasping that He loves you, in response to His love work in a way that worships and glorifies Him.

Q: What does this idea of a theology of work mean for a person who has a physical or cognitive disability or any special need?

A: First let's clarify that work is not necessarily synonymous with a job. While a theology of work warrants discussion of careers, the larger topic of work involves all of the endeavors to which we devote ourselves. Work does not fit in one category that only individuals with certain physical or cognitive abilities can embrace.

> The bigger concept a theology of work emphasizes is to dedicate whatever energy and commitments we have to God with sensitivity to His direction and to perform as an offering of worship to Him. Scripture leaves the description of such endeavors open to anything:
>
> "Whatever your hand finds to do, do it with your might" (Ecclesiastes 9:10).
>
> "And whatever you do, do it heartily, as to the Lord and not to men" (Colossians 3:23).

Look at those twelve grasshoppers from Numbers 13 again. They were put to work for forty days with a mission to spy and report. It was more than a job; it was a special mission bigger than they grasped. Could it be that their choices were a result of their misunderstanding of their mission, or at least their failure to approach their work with a right spirit and mindset?

Work encompasses not just what you do in formal roles at church or for livelihood but all areas of service. Grasshoppers were made to serve; after all, we were made in the image of God. Thus Brand and Yancey challenge:

> Radical Christians who urge action in the inner city, politically conservative Christians who give large sums of their investments to missions, seminary students who glory in their new-found knowledge, church members who fill out committees within the church—all of us need to come back to the image of the Son of God kneeling on a hard floor and unbuckling sandals covered with choking Palestine dust. We cannot find real fulfillment by demonstrating individual strength as a

muscle unit in Christ's Body. Rather, our activity
must be for the sake of the Body.[10]

From speaking the cosmos into existence to shaping the first human with His own hand to stooping before His followers to wash
their feet, our God works. As we seek to be conformed to His
image, we too will work—not to gain His love or build our own material kingdom but to honor Him and serve others. One Christian
scholar put it in perspective: "Work is the form in which we make
ourselves useful to others. . . . That is why work gives meaning to
life . . . through work that serves others, we also serve God."[11]

That bay mare with the prized pedigree is roaming in a pasture somewhere. She's isolated and just being a horse, all because
she didn't have the right approach to work. Instead of learning
from the industrious ant, in this case we learn from the horse with
wasted potential.

Today you have the opportunity to let God reprogram you to
see work in a new way. You can see it as a way to honor God and to
serve others. While the rest of the world despises the boss, jockeys
for position in the rat race, or sits out to protest the system in general, as a child of God made in His image, we can reflect the glory
of God in everything to which we give our energy.

QUESTIONS FOR REFLECTION

- What project or commitment gets most of your energy? Can you say that your efforts honor God? If not, how could those commitments be modified to do so?
- What motivates you to work? A paycheck? A certain grade? The next vacation? Just getting through to the weekend?
- What would your work look like if you recalibrated your motives with the goal of giving God glory in all your endeavors and commitments?

PRAYER

God, thank You that You are a God at work—in creating us and in caring for us still today. In Your image, we want to be workers who honor You and bring You glory in all we do. I ask You today to speak to me about areas of my life where I need to purify my motives. Call me to projects that are a testimony to Your greatness, and strengthen me to work. Thank you for this privilege, Jesus.

CHAPTER 14

GRASSHOPPERS WERE BORN TO DREAM

grew up at a time when you could get a driver's license the day you turned fifteen. What that meant was that you started practicing when you were fourteen. And so when I was fourteen, my parents started teaching me to drive. I still remember that overwhelming feeling of staring over the steering wheel and trying to get my bearings. It was terrifying, and I felt tiny. A bit like a grasshopper.

We had a two-tone blue and tan Ford pickup—a three-quarter ton with a long-wheel base. That poor truck. If it's still remotely intact in some distant junkyard, it bears the scars of the abuse I gave it during my fifteenth year of life.

On one particular day, my dad and I were working inside the barn and he asked me to go get the truck up at the house and drive it to the barn so we could unload feed. Eager to get behind the wheel and enjoy the coolness that was driving (wow, didn't that fade fast?) I bounded off for the house. Between the barn and the house is a riding corral. My job was to drive the truck up the driveway by the house, through the gate leading into the riding corral, through the corral, and up to the gate connecting the barn and the corral.

When I got to the truck, I noticed a trailer was sitting in the driveway in front of the corral. There was a space between the truck and the corral gate. An engineer I was not, but I inspected the space and deduced that I couldn't fit the truck around the trailer and into the gate. I trotted back to the barn to report to my dad.

Apparently I was not a communicator any more than I was an engineer. I cannot remember the words I used, but I expressed some measure of concern about getting the truck through the small space of the gate. I am still not sure what words my dad heard, and I am still not sure why I did not plainly articulate there was a trailer in front of the gate. If you ever had a Stark's or a Ward's or even a Dairy Queen in your town and lost a quarter to the Frogger arcade game, you could get a picture for what I was up against. However, my dad assured me I could get through the gate and sent me back for the truck a second time with a bit more urgency.

I appreciate that in my house we never got in trouble for trying. Had that not been the case, the rest of the story would be an uncomfortable memory. As it was, I angled the pickup at the trajectory that best seemed to shoot the rapids, as it were, around the trailer and into the narrow corral gate. The crunch that greeted me seconds later and sent my dad sprinting out of the barn confirmed my original deduction.

This is not necessarily a book about communication, so I'll leave those lessons learned for another time. But what blows my mind even now about that incident (and unfortunately at least two other similar stories) is how my dad calmly handled the situation as if all part of the plan. I put that poor pickup, a Buick, and a Honda Civic through what can only be described as a precursor to the opening of the seals in Revelation, and never once did my dad get angry or ridicule me for trying to learn. I also remember being embarrassed and discouraged after each new incident and wanting to quit. I remember specifically asking my parents if I could just not get my driver's license I was so ready to give up.

I hate to break this news if you're still clinging to hope otherwise, but I have to tell you that we're going to mess up in life, in ministry, in relationships, and in anything else we try. But God forms His grasshoppers with purpose in mind, and resident in that purpose are dreams. Unfortunately dreams worth dreaming are usually difficult to realize. But just as I was fortunate to learn from my earthly father as a young teen, our heavenly Father is not rattled by our missteps and failures. When He puts a dream in your heart and nudges you out of the nest, He is going to be waiting patiently to fix your oops-a-daisies and put you right back in the driver's seat to try again.

Yes, God's gifts don't just come in the form of skillsets and talents; He also gifts us with the ability to dream. Dreamers are those who influenced human history and whose stories we still celebrate today. It's not just that we like their stories, though we do; God likes dreamers. He made them and He filled the Bible with them.

The go-to Sunday school story involves the ultimate dreamer: Joseph. It's just a car chase short of prime-time drama. A young man has dreams, and everything blows up from there.

Joseph is unusual because he didn't struggle from the grasshopper effect of thinking himself insignificant or ruling out God's vision. Instead of thinking himself small, he dreamed that his family bowed to him. And his brothers got angry at that vision of a peer being more important than they were.

You know the rest of the story. The dreamer prevailed because the God who gave the dreams came through despite ridiculous odds. God is the hero in the story, but Joseph gets honorable mention for holding to the faith that the Dreamgiver was worth trusting.

Throughout Scripture God gave dreams to His people. Sometimes those dreams came in dramatic visual fashion of prophetic revelation such as Jacob's dream of a ladder to Heaven and the assurance He would receive Abraham's promise (Genesis 28:10–17) or the New Testament's Joseph's angelic visitation in a dream to announce his role in the Savior's birth (Matthew 1:20; 2:13). Still other times God simply whispered a direction, or a dream, into the heart of His child—and not always the most qualified and promising candidates. Isn't that what spurred four men with leprosy to get up and do something—in their case to march into the enemy camp (II Kings 7:3–16)? We could debate whether or not the impulse originated from self or from God, but the results speak for themselves: God honored their motivation, divinely multiplied the sound of their footsteps into that of an army, and used their action to dispel the enemy and save the starving Israelites. Maybe our dreams today will come in dramatic visual form or maybe in the tiny spark of a tentative plan, but God is still imparting divine direction and motivation to do something for His kingdom for those who will shirk off grasshopper perspectives of doubt and insecurity and embrace the vision God inspires.

Understanding that we are made in God's image involves accepting the dreams and creative abilities God intends for us. Consider it this way: "We received a divine imprint that left us with qualities that resemble our Creator. One of those divinely imparted qualities is creativity . . . [God] left His imprint on us. Much like a craftsman's work often reflects his own character and nature, God imparted His creative ability to us. It should not seem strange that we are recipients of this ability to create, for God Himself was indeed the Creator."[1] Lewis and Demarest add:

> Because we are, like God, transcendent spiritual beings, we have some ability and responsibility to work, think, speak, and write with *creativity*. We can compare and combine things differently, and imagine and propose new ways of doing things. . . . When humans wisely use these cognitive capacities, they produce cultures and subcultures with their distinctive types of art, music, architecture, horticulture, literature, religions, and mores. Like God, people have a capacity for creative imagination, goalsetting, strategies, and actions. Artists, sculptors, architects, writers, and many others have enriched our lives by creatively developing fresh approaches. We may need courage to exercise our creative capacities to develop different strategies and methods for advancing God's universal and redemptive kingdoms.[2]

Almost nothing is as potent and world-changing as a child of God with a dream. Whether in the form of a specific idea or general creativity, willingness to dream opens endless possibilities to work for God's kingdom.

We must strive to grow from an insecure grasshopper to a God-inspired dreamer. First we must learn to balance the passion of the dream with wisdom. It's easy and tempting to make Joseph the martyr and his brothers the monsters, and certainly God's favor was with Joseph and He ordained everything in His life for good. But could Joseph have handled his dream with more care along the way? Though it was all used by God, does not the reaction of his brothers teach us the prayerful wisdom we must use in sharing our dreams? Dreams in isolation sometimes don't work because God usually gives us a dream for a purpose, and His purpose usually involves the community of people He created. So we need to share our dreams, but how a dreamer shares the dream with others must be saturated with prayer, wisdom, and humility.

Yet we mustn't be afraid to dream. Don't be afraid to try. God is the giver of dreams, and as we seek our identity, purpose, and gifts from Him, He will whisper dreams. We must trust the Dreamgiver to carry out in our lives whatever He promises. Dale Carnegie used to teach that one way to overcome fear and anxiety was to ask yourself, "What is the worst that can possibly happen?" to identify your fear, compartmentalize it, and then think about how you would move on past it.[3] I don't want to mix popular culture's version of advice with our biblical mandates, but I think stopping to ask ourselves what we fear can help us put everything in perspective. When we are in God's hand pursuing the dream He placed in our hearts, what's the worst that can happen? I assure you it's nothing He can't handle and nothing worth quitting over (Romans 8:31).

Even if your dream is bigger than you feel you are, trust in the Dreamgiver. You may feel like a grasshopper in comparison, but He is big enough to pull it off. Your dream may not look like anyone else's and that's okay. The same God who handcrafted you with unique DNA and a unique thumbprint has given you a unique dream for a unique purpose. You can trust Him.

Finally, we must pray for the wisdom and patience to put the dream in action. And this is the part of the story I don't like, but I must tell it. Joseph's dream didn't happen overnight—not even close. It included being sold as a slave and a stint in the Pen. I would like to tell you that your dream comes with a negotiable timeline but that's not the case. What I can tell you is that dreamers who cast off grasshopper insecurities are sustained by a God who is just as real in the prison as He is in the palace. Stay faithful. Pray for wisdom and patience. Remember that just as the Dreamgiver didn't mean for you to dream grasshopper dreams, He doesn't intend to leave you, no matter where your dreams take you.

QUESTIONS FOR REFLECTION

- Have you ever felt God was revealing to you what purpose He wanted to carry out in your life?
- What steps have you taken to pursue that dream?
- If you are struggling to find a dream and a direction, what can you do to position yourself in a posture to hear from God?

PRAYER

Lord Jesus, I thank You that You hold my future in Your hand—the same hand that holds all of the universe and yet that is nail-scarred for me. I am humbled that You love me and that You trust me to do a work for Your kingdom. I ask You, Jesus, to put a dream in my heart of what You want to do with my life. I commit myself to trusting You to bring to pass what You have promised. Please give me wisdom and patience to pursue this dream You have given me.

CHAPTER 15

GRASSHOPPERS WITH EARS

Contrary to what many people probably assume, grasshoppers and locusts don't use their antennae for hearing, but rather ears (tympanum) on their abdomens. I am almost embarrassed I know that. It borders on the obsessive, and to be sure most people with wi-fi as temperamental as mine wouldn't squander it on insect research. However, I have found it strangely fascinating to discover the intricacies of grasshopper anatomy. Did you know that the complexity of the directional hearing grasshoppers possess rivals that of humans?[1] Until the middle of the nineteenth century, we didn't even know grasshoppers could hear. I'm not sure who or how someone made the discovery, but it turns out hearing is critical for insects to avoid predators, detect prey, and find mates—in a word: survive.

When I thought we had the blueprint for this book complete, Joel called me and said we had missed something. When he began to explain, I had to admit he was right: we had let prayer become an afterthought.

We can't talk about human identity without talking about the privilege of communicating with God. It is not only our means of survival, but it is a gift from God to facilitate the relationship with Him we were designed for. That gift, that opportunity, shapes and directs every other area of our lives.

Like with insects, hearing on a spiritual level is vital for us to survive and thrive. Scripture speaks of "ears to hear" in several places. Three of the Gospels recount Jesus' admonition that those with ears should hear (Matthew 11:15; Mark 4:9, 29; Luke 8:8). Again in Revelation as John dictated special messages for the seven churches, each message ended with a call to hear what the Spirit would say to the church (Revelation 2:7, 11, 17, 29; 3:6, 13, 22).

This plea of Scripture always puzzled me as a child. Who doesn't have ears? Is it a rhetorical question? When I sit in a church service and sense a minister appealing with fervency to a congregation, I wonder if in those moments we realize Scripture's call to hear is not rhetorical but more real and more urgent than any other voice influencing our lives. The voices we choose to listen to decide our future.

Take Abraham. We know him as the great patriarch who became the father of many nations and the namesake of the world's greatest Sunday school song. Ever. But it was not always thus. Abraham was a polytheistic pagan in a place called Ur where his family worshiped idols. And then one day a God he'd never heard of called him to abandon his hometown, his family, and his inheritance to embark toward an undisclosed location with further directions to follow.

What would possess a well-settled man to take such a drastic leap of faith? Well, just that: faith. I wonder if Abraham felt something akin to the exciting presence of God you've felt in those special times when God touched you in a deeply personal way. Or

I wonder if there were no goosebumps and butterflies but there was something sovereign and trustworthy in that voice much like the clarity and credence we sense when we read God's Word? Whatever the case, Abraham chose to enter that special covenant freely—God did not coerce him but called him, illustrating a unique aspect of how God created humanity: with ears to hear God's call and the free will to choose. Apostolic scholar David Norris put it this way: "Covenant relationship with the Creator is constituted and sustained by human response. Unfortunately, Adam and Eve, created in the image of God, did not choose to keep covenant. There were certainly consequences of their disobedience—the loss of Eden, thorns, pain, death, and more—consequences that are still with us. . . . In every generation humanity must make the same choice made by Adam and Eve, whether or not to be in relationship with God."[2] Grace is extended, but we have the volition to accept it. That's what makes us humans and not God's robots. Just like those original grasshoppers, we have ears to hear God's offer of covenant relationship, and just like them we must decide our response. Like them, every single aspect of our future depends on it.

Let's bear down on what makes us who we are. This is no small discussion. With fervor that makes the greatest of sports rivalries look petty, theologians have been debating and refining anthropology—the study of humanity—as long as they have been studying the doctrine of God Himself. Irenaeus and several other early religious thinkers emphasized the power we have as humans to think, arguing intellect was what indicated we were made in God's image—being able to use reason in a way superior to any other created being. Certainly there is credence to that viewpoint. But other theologians would point out that defining humans as simply rational overlooks the emotive side of our identity as well, leaving the issue of human ontology, or nature of being, incomplete.[3]

It would be nice if God had etched on a stone in Ten-Commandments-style font a recipe or simple formula for what makes a human human. In the absence of such an ingredients list, we continue to theologize. Some passages of Scripture suggest the basic elements of our humanity are body, spirit, and soul (Hebrews 4:12; I Thessalonians 5:23).[4] But unlike other anthropology texts that would hyperfocus on dissecting these parts and speculating on the way these elements homogenize, let's put it all in perspective: whether we are human because we have an intellect or because we have a soul or emotions or any combination of those elements, what matters is that we surrender all of who we are to God.

To be human is to worship something. Spiritual ears to hear God's call goes hand in hand with the reality that we were born to worship. By worship, I don't mean the twenty-one minutes of a church service where we clap along to music and bob our heads. Every part of our lives was meant to be lived in adoration and communion with the loving God who handcrafted us. One scholar articulated a three-part definition of worship: "(1) divine initiation in which God graciously reveals himself, his purposes, and will; (2) a spiritual and personal relationship with God . . . (3) a response by the worshiper of joyful adoration, reverence, humility, submission and obedience."[5] Simply put: all of life is worship, and we're all worshiping something. As grasshoppers designed in God's image, we are called to worship Him in totality.

The *Shema*, the basis of the Old Covenant and the heart of the Hebrew Law still revered by Jews today, proclaims: "You shall love the Lord your God with all your heart, with all your soul, and with all your strength" (Deuteronomy 6:5). When the scribes questioned Jesus about the greatest commandment, He quoted the

Shema. Lewis and Demarest explain, "A person's highest duty is to 'love the Lord your God with all your heart [*kardia*] and with all your soul [*psyche*] and with all your mind [*dianoia*],' Mark 12:30 and Luke 10:27 add a fourth word, 'strength' (*ischys*). Each of these Greek words signify different aspects of the person's inner life—the aggregate of terms underscoring the totality of love due to God."[6] We're closest to God, yielded and conformed most tightly to His image, when we are intentional in reverent, whole-hearted pursuit of Him.

My submission that we have the privilege to pursue relationship directly with God may seem like a given to some, but for thousands of years various religions have inserted intermediaries and established a gulf between humanity and deity. Scripture gives us a far better way: "Let us therefore come boldly to the throne of grace" (Hebrews 4:16). Though He is Creator, Sovereign Ruler, Master, King, and every other deified attribute our brain can process, He permits—invites—us to boldly come into His presence as heirs instead of paupers.

This privilege engenders a special communion with Him that challenges my abilities to describe it. One writer explains, "As spirits in God's image, furthermore, we can transcend our consciousness of self, the world, and others and become *God-conscious*. The divine presence is not far from any one of us."[7] In this beautiful process of communion, God not only hears us but also communicates to us. "The ability to see spiritual principles is closely related to our receptivity to them and our readiness to act upon them. Unfortunately these abilities and desires may be decimated by sinful desires. Nevertheless, a general illumination enables all to know God's existence, power, and righteous demands."[8] Even this description falls short of describing the glorious presence of God we can experience firsthand in an intimate way. You simply must take advantage of the invitation yourself to understand.

A few decades ago a surgeon and a Christian writer teamed up to author an extended study of how the church compares to a physical body. They articulated something profound: "It is a brilliant stroke, the only pure egalitarianism I observe in all of society. [God] has endowed every person in the Body with the same capacity to respond to Him."[9] All of us have an invitation to hear God's whisper to commune with Him.

Joel tells of his early years in ministry. He left an exciting career in the horse industry and began assisting with the maintenance for the district campground. With a new facility, Joel wore a number of hats and threw himself into everything from operating equipment to appliance repairs and any number of roles in between. His wife, Jessica, is a gifted organizer, and the two focused on being assets to the church in service and administration.

Some time later, as Joel began serving as youth pastor at his church, he recognized he was not necessarily like other student pastors who perhaps spent time learning teen buzzwords and staying current on popular culture topics that were trending. Human moments occurred from time to time that made him wonder if his ministry to students was impeded by not focusing more on being a trendy, relevant youth minister. But he chose to focus on what he believed were the gifts God had placed in his life and work in the areas of service God had presented.

During that time Joel began to minister to a young lady named Clarissa[10] who was overcoming a difficult past that included family homicide, and she was at an intersection of life-changing decisions. He remembers a time Clarissa sat with tears running down her face, grappling with the past and desperate for direction. Clarissa didn't need the maintenance man; she didn't need an air conditioner serviced. Changing a light bulb or organizing an engaging event wasn't going to help her. She also didn't need a trendy youth pastor who knew the lyrics to the most popular songs. She needed someone who could hear from God. That moment gave Joel a fresh revelation: being Spirit-led to hear from God and minister to lives is the most needful focus. We must be led by Him to lead others.

Your talents are gifts from God; this book acknowledges and celebrates that. Yes, we were made to dream and, yes, we were made to work. But our kingdom work is subject to being in communication with God. Maybe you see yourself as insignificant or maybe you only see yourself with one label: "I'm the maintenance guy. I'm the gal who plans great events." These labels aren't the ones that matter. Your only identity that matters is what God gives. That comes from hearing His whisper in a time of prayer. To circumvent pride or insecurity—either of which can hinder your ability to make an impact—turn your focus to the greatest gift you have: the privilege to hear from Him, be led of His Spirit, and be used of Him to minister to others.

QUESTIONS FOR REFLECTION

- When is the last time you felt like God spoke to you or impressed something to you?
- When is the last time you lost yourself in an intimate place of worship in God's presence?
- If you can't think of recent times as answers to those questions, what could you do to position yourself in a place to communicate more intimately with God?
- What does your ideal prayer life look like? How can you get there?

PRAYER

Father, there is nothing more important to me than walking in covenant relationship with You. I know that You have called me graciously and given me the free choice to serve You. I want to tell You again in a fresh way today, Lord, that I want You and I need You. I recommit to a life of worship and daily time of prayer in Your presence. Thank You for that privilege of prayer. Thank You for the promise I have that You will meet me there. Give me a fresh sensitivity to Your whisper. In Jesus' name, amen.

CHAPTER 16

ONE GRASSHOPPER AMONG MANY

D id you know that each summer, typically around May or June, pet lovers celebrate International Hug Your Cat Day? On that day those special people who keep up with offbeat celebrations popularized by the Internet will give their cat a hug—provided, of course, the evil creature allows them to do so. I have to confess the insolence and general air of superiority of cats rubs me the wrong way. But for probably dozens of people this is a grand day. One website claims the day is "the perfect opportunity to put your cat on a pedestal and thank her for all those times she has curled up next to you after a long day."[1]

Despite my grumpiness and general reticence toward cats, I appreciate the sentiment and I recognize the very real need we have as humans for affection. In fact, I would submit to you some of our devotion to pets is symptomatic of our larger need for human care and compassion.

I once read the story of Sharon, a researcher who shared her experience in *Psychology Today*. Sharon is a brilliant woman; she holds a PhD in social work from New York University, has authored two books, travels to speaking engagements all over the country to talk about mental health, and operates a successful psychotherapy practice. But when Sharon's mom passed away, some things began to happen that Sharon couldn't explain with all her vast education and training.[2]

Sharon's shoulder began to freeze up. Always a sound sleeper, she found herself waking up in the night, unable to sleep because of the pain. Sharon went to the doctor, but he couldn't help her. He found no scar tissue, no nerve damage, no bone-alignment issues: simply put, doctors had no medical explanation for Sharon's pain.

So Sharon started physical therapy. Something unusual happened when Sharon went to her first session. When the therapist began to treat Sharon's shoulder, the sensation of physical touch and the act of being cared for drew out of Sharon an emotional response. She began to cry, and she began to think of her mom, and Sharon began the grieving process.

Over the next several months, Sharon discovered what doctors and psychologists cannot explain but have come to understand: sometimes emotional pain manifests itself physically in the body for no other seeming purpose than to bring about personal interaction and the act of being cared for. Scientists have theories about what hormones may be released that create bonds of affection or feelings of love and attachment, which ultimately point to this submission: human beings need affection, compassion, and care from other human beings.

Now you wouldn't think it would take scientists and psychologists millions of dollars and years of research to arrive at that profound truth that many of us as caring human beings know instinctively, but it's amazing how easy it is to overlook this fundamental truth of who we are. Until the 1920s the United States had a staggering infant mortality rate in foundling hospitals. When physicians finally tried the novel idea of including touch in their care, the infant mortality rate decreased significantly.[3] Our need for physical human touch is astounding.

If you think about it, our culture is pulling us apart. Both my mother and grandmother grew up on farms where the nearest neighbor might live forty or more acres away. I live less than forty feet from my neighbor. But relationally, I don't know my neighbors anywhere close to the way my mother and grandmother knew theirs. Robert D. Putnam's book in 2000 on the disintegration of the American social fabric in the last half of the twentieth century disturbed us as he presented the very simple phenomenon that people are isolating themselves due to any number of factors from work to media to generational change.[4] With the explosion of social media in the twenty-first century, we're dashing head-long into increasingly separate and isolated lives. The front porch has largely disappeared. Used to be, at least in the South, folks spent the evening on their front porches to keep up with what was happening in the community and talk with any neighbors who stopped. These days, we get through our work day, fight to keep our sanity among the road-rage of the interstate, go home to lock the door, and drown out the day with entertainment and social media.[5]

North Americans generally embrace and even celebrate the idea of rugged individualism and independence. While I honor our forefathers and am thankful for our political freedoms, I recognize that if we take this same approach to the way we live our lives and relationships—"I don't need any help; I can do it myself; I don't need anyone"—we overlook something fundamental in the way God wired us to operate.

We know that the Bible is unified, is sound, and when submitted to the scrutiny of study, presents a clear picture of who God is and His incredible plan throughout history to be in relationship with humanity. And yet there are these fascinating tensions in Scripture. God is perfect and holy and yet He can have mercy on me in my imperfections. God is all-knowing and yet He chooses to remember my sins no more. And here's a key one that fascinates me: God calls us into a personal relationship and yet He puts us into a body of other believers. The Bible says to "work out your own salvation"—you can't outsource your personal response to Jesus' call to you to be in relationship with Him. I can't decide that for you and you can't decide it for me. My response to salvation is my decision alone. Yet once we respond to the New Testament example of repentance, baptism, and receiving His Spirit, we are made members of a worldwide, mighty, and majestic body or family.[6] First Corinthians 12:13 establishes that "by one Spirit are we all baptized into one body, whether we be Jews or Gentiles." Whoever we are, wherever we are from—when we enter a relationship with Jesus Christ, we also enter a relationship with every other believer. This "body of believers" is the church. I'm not just talking about a local building, although that's important, but "the called out" people who are in relationship with God and are in turn in relationship with one another.

Let's dive deeper into theological waters for a moment. Part of what it means to bear the image of God is to be wired for relationship. Based on the idea that God can't be understood as a thing ("it") but a person ("Thou"), theologians like Karl Barth and Emil Brunner argue: "Persons are image-bearers of God because they are capable of sustaining a broad range of 'I-Thou' relationships."[7] Other thinkers have argued, "God Himself saw the need to come alongside us, not just love us at a distance. How could He fully manifest love except through Human flesh? . . . Together we can fulfill God's command to fill the earth with His presence and love. When we stretch out our hand to help, we stretch out the hand of

Christ's Body."[8] This book is essentially an Apostolic anthropology (the study of humans), and we couldn't get far down that path without crossing into ecclesiology (the study of the church). Scripture uses metaphors to describe this body of believers including the example of the church as a building or temple (fitly framed together—Ephesians 2:19–22), as a family (we are all God's children so we are all brothers and sisters—explaining why you'll hear us emphasize "sister" and "brother" when we greet each other), and as a body.

A body has many parts and they all have to work in sync. If the organs begin to attack one another, we know the body is sick. But when the body is working as it was designed, the body can accomplish incredible feats. One of the things the body can do is heal itself. If the body is functioning properly and you suffer a cut, the blood cells will coagulate. Over time the skin will close and the tissue will mend. If the church, the family of followers of Jesus, is like a body, there are times the body can heal itself. I don't want to abuse that analogy. We know that healing for physical or emotional needs comes from Jesus, and people all around the globe can testify of His healing power. He is our healer—first and foremost. But sometimes He chooses to use the body to minister to others in the body to be part of that healing process.

All of us will have times where we just need to get alone with God and dig in and get answers from Him—times where we need personal, deep, intimate interaction in a consecrated time of prayer where God moves on us supernaturally. Absolutely those times are in order. But there are also times when the body—the corporate group of members—is to care for one another. We should be so closely connected as a family that when one of us hurts, all of us hurt. When one of us is blessed, all of us feel blessed.

That kind of thinking is counter-cultural. We have songs and TV shows and games built around the idea of being a "survivor"—the idea that by my own strength and wit and ingenuity, I can handle things all by myself. In a world where we compete on jobs for promotions and our kids compete against each other for top spots in sports, this kind of interconnectedness, deeper than even family ties, flies in the face of everything our society wires us to expect. But that's exactly how the Word of God describes the church: "There should be no schism in the body, but that the members should have the same care for one another. And if one member suffers, all the members suffer with it; or if one member is honored, all the members rejoice with it" (I Corinthians 12:25–26). That kind of connectedness is not just counter-cultural, it's against our human nature.

How old are children when they begin to say "I do it! I do it by myself"? Just as we don't want to need God's grace, we also don't want to need help from others. I don't want to need anyone. I hate depending on people. I want to be strong and independent and tough enough to handle things on my own. My pride doesn't want me to look weak or vulnerable, and so I resist going to a peer or an elder and saying, "I have a problem. I need help."

Asking for help is not a weakness; that's a God-designed impulse to help the church be the church. Scriptures fill the New Testament where the church is instructed to "comfort one another," "encourage each other," "build up," and "care for the body" (Galatians 6:2; I Thessalonians 5:11; James 5:16). God uses the body to show His love to us.

If you will walk the aisles of your local church, you should be able to find person after person who can tell a story about how God came through and did something miraculous that defied the very laws of nature. That testimony is meant to be shared. I have hope that I can make it through my problems because there are other people surrounding me who have told me how God helped them make it through their problems.

All over your church there should be people God has used to minister to others in difficult times. For me it's walking up to the altar at fourteen years old, feeling God and having no idea what to do with it, and Sister Paula Cryer coming up and praying with me, helping me learn to seek God in what was one of the most powerful times of prayer in my life. It's the conversations I had with my pastors that gave me the hope to believe God could use me in ministry. It's a snapshot that's sealed in my mind of Sister Oden and Sister Soileau in our church kitchen lovingly preparing food for a family having a funeral—the church being the church, the body caring for the body. God ministered to me in those moments, and He used my brothers and sisters to do it. We are meant to be connected to others, caring for one another.

How is the church any different than a support group or a community charity club? The difference is that we recognize this body, this bringing together of very different people to be so intimately interconnected, is orchestrated by God and depends entirely on Him. Jesus Christ is the head of this body, and we are people of His name. When we care for one another in His name and with the empowerment of His Spirit, this body can experience miraculous things we can never see in our human abilities and limitations. It gives us a hope that no matter how bad our personal situations are, there is a God who is bigger. It gives us assurance that no matter how inadequate I feel to encourage you or help you when you're in trouble, I'm directed and empowered by a great big God who can lead me to minister to you.

Those ten spies in Numbers 13 flipped out when they saw the enemy and labeled themselves as grasshoppers. What they overlooked was that when one grasshopper joins with another grasshopper and then they join with more grasshoppers and on and on, a militia is assembled. An army of grasshoppers can level vegetation and displace entire communities. Imagine if the original grasshoppers had only envisioned their power to unite as the army God intended. Imagine if the church of today would only envision our power to unite as the caring body God intends.

QUESTIONS FOR REFLECTION

- How closely are you connected to other believers outside of your own home and family?
- Are you trying to manage problems or shoulder burdens on your own? Why or why not?
- How sensitive and responsive are you to God's voice so He can use you to minister to someone if a need arises in the body of Christ?
- Are you willing to follow the leading of His Spirit if He gives you a verse of Scripture to share with someone or a word of encouragement?

PRAYER

Mighty God, I thank You today for calling me into relationship with You. I realize that when You saved me, You intended for me not just to be connected to You, but to be part of a family—connected to all the believers You have called to follow You. Jesus, today give me the courage to open my heart to my brothers and sisters. Help me to realize my need for the body of Christ. Give me the courage to share my needs with the church for prayer and for help. Father, I ask that You would also give me the sensitivity and the compassion to care for other believers around me. We are all Your people, and I want us to be the family You have called us to be.

CHAPTER 17

GRASSHOPPERS UNDER A MAGNIFYING GLASS

What did those spies in Numbers 13 see when they looked in the mirror? It must not have been much given the evil report they shared. Perhaps the more telling question is what they thought others saw when they looked at them. The answer, of course, is grasshoppers (Numbers 13:33). They assumed their enemy thought so too. Why did those grasshoppers worry so much about the enemy's opinion?

Lest we think ourselves somehow superior to those grasshoppers, let's be real: this age-old problem of worrying about what others think of us still preys on all our minds. It's why the advertising industry exists: to convince us of what we need based on how it will make us feel in comparison to others. You can even see it in the nonconformist who dresses outlandishly—so he can look like every other nonconformist.

We can fold our hands and tsk-tsk at those poor insecure souls who let the rest of the world dictate the way they dress and the toys they buy. Yet isn't it just as sad and taxing when rather than being influenced by others we try to influence others to think of us in a certain way?

Wayne Cordeiro's description of "image management" captures a condition all humans grapple with though we may never consciously put it into words like Cordeiro has.[1] Image management refers to our human efforts to control the perception the world has of us. Though that definition is somewhat contradictory since we cannot control another person, in our desire for others to perceive good evaluations of us (perhaps out of prideful motives and perhaps simply the reality of our humanity), we try to project an outside image that would impress others. Cordeiro diagnoses his image management efforts in contrast to his own inner turmoil, suggesting when we focus more on image management than on stewarding not our image but our true lives, we run aground.

Who can't identify with Cordeiro's efforts to manage his image? Who doesn't want others to think well of them? In a different context, the Bible even mentions not letting others speak evil of our good (Romans 14:16). But protecting our reputation or avoiding actions that cause others to stumble is a far cry from simply being the servant God has called us to be. If we're hyperfocused on personal promotion, then we're not understanding and living out the Apostolic identity God intends for us. In my life I find that when I get out of balance and attempt image management, it is usually a result of not aligning myself with the purpose God has intended for me. When I remind myself He is the only one I need to please and He will provide whatever needs I have without my having to win the affections of others, it puts this all in perspective.

If this book hasn't said it lately, let me be clear: only God gets to define your worth. Somehow you must reach the point of living for an audience of One. It means shutting off the voices of a society that says you're too [fill in the blank] and not comparing ourselves with one another. Is it no wonder that on the heels of talking about the battle between the flesh and the spirit and the understanding that we are God's, Paul urged the church: "For we dare not class ourselves or compare ourselves with those who commend themselves. But they, measuring themselves by themselves, and comparing themselves among themselves, are not wise" (II Corinthians 10:12). Recent writers have shared an admonition specific to young adults: "Comparing yourself to others and attempting to measure up to society's standards will do nothing but leave you feeling incomplete. You are not valued and defined by what others assume; you are designed and defined by God."[2] Every age level of the church must grasp this vital biblical principle. Our life is authored by God, and He doesn't mean for the fate of your story to be subject to the critics. You are who He says you are, and your life should reflect the peace and security of that revelation.

It's impossible to talk about our being secure in our God-given identity and its implications without acknowledging the pressures that have been added with the advent of social media. It probably reveals a little something about my age, but as I work with students and young adults, I've caught myself frequently remarking to friends how glad I am I didn't grow up with social media. Mistakes I made in the past are basically limited to old friends from high school and college who I imagine have mercifully closed out the past as the past. Today's youth broadcast impulsive thoughts and pictures without the advantage of reflection and that instant transmission forges their impetuous mistakes on the minds of a wide, fickle audience. It's image management on a whole new level, and it's scary.

*   *   *   *   *

I love to fish. At some point it's downright weird how much I enjoy it, but those guys in the Bible did a lot of fishing, so I tell myself I'm in good company. One of the 3,812 reasons I like fishing is because of the time we spend together as a family. We have an understood routine every time we take the boat out: my mother pays for the launch and bait while my dad and I ready the boat. It's normally a straightforward process, but recently we experienced a hiccup in our well-oiled routine.

With the boat launched, the rods ready, and quiet marshes as far the eye could see beckoning, Mom was still nowhere in sight. My dad and I waited as patiently in the boat as we were capable, which probably meant about 0.00174 seconds, and we hopped out to start the search party.

As these stories go, just at that moment when we gave up, out the marina door bounded Mom. She was eager to tell us her story.

I should pause here and say that another of the 3,812 reasons I like fishing is because every trip to Louisiana is a cultural bazaar. The marina owner my mom met would be a star attraction. When Mom stepped up in the line to buy bait, he quickly discerned that she was not up-to-date on the status of a freshwater diversion measure being proposed by state legislators with the potential to worsen erosion for saltwater coasts. Over the course of the next ten minutes, he gave her an evangelistic sermon on the matter with a fervor that preachers the world over would be proud to attain.

He did such a good job my mom signed a petition on the spot and brought me and my dad information on how to do our part for the cause. I'm not much of a protestor, so I missed the finer points of the tutorial and didn't sign the petition myself. Yet the more I've thought about it, the more I have become curious about the issue itself: the phenomenon of erosion. You can stare at a shoreline all day long and not see erosion, but two satellite photos of that same shoreline taken fifteen years apart can reveal startling loss.

The metaphor of erosion grips me as I think of the change in our sense of community and in the way social media could be distorting our sense of who we are as individuals and as a community. As times change and the rural roots of North America grow more distant with the commercialization of the farming industry and urbanization, perhaps as we grow closer in geographical proximity, our social bonds are weakening. Additionally, in the United States single adults now outnumber married couples, according to a study reported by *The New York Post* in 2014.³ Whatever the causes of this change in American demographics, the results could include increased isolation as well as weakening values surrounding relationships.

Amid these sociological factors, we must consider the role of technology. It would be easy to jump on the bandwagon that technology is the root cause of all evils, but what specifically is its effect on community? Is technology one of the causes of weakened community, or a symptom of larger cultural conditions? Only the reports of sociologists twenty or fifty years from now will be able to answer that question definitively, but in the meantime, we can identify what aspects of social media are problematic and set guardrails to prevent further erosion of our relational and community values.

One reason social media becomes a substitute for face-to-face relationships is that it fosters a false sense of intimacy in an idealistic virtual world. The term "online disinhibition" describes how the lack of face-to-face communication erodes inhibitions, enabling people to communicate things more extremely and sooner than they would in person. It also explains why a fourteen year old or forty year old can abandon her family to be with her "soulmate" she met online five weeks before. Relationships of any kind suffer from a lack of inhibitions, and given this phenomenon of online disinhibitions, our virtual relationship-building is plagued with significant threats.

Another negative effect of social media is that it creates unrealistic expectations of what life should be and pressure to create artificial broadcasts to project an appealing life that wins followers—a problematic form of image management. Author Jaron Lanier, whose book *You Are Not a Gadget* critiques Facebook's tendency to foster self-presentation, explains: "I fear that we are beginning to design ourselves to suit digital models of us, and I worry about a leaching of empathy and humanity in that process."[4] If Lanier's fears are true and social media forces us into broadcasting mode, the implications are that our sense of reality and legitimate relationships could be eroded, not to mention the extreme narcissism it promotes. Do we know how to be ourselves or are we too busy trying to create a life worthy of our broadcast audience's "likes?"

Those kind of research possibilities scare me in the face of our identity crises. It's one thing to talk about having a healthy identity and avoiding the extremes of a Goliath arrogance or beat-down grasshopper insecurities. It's another thing to apply hypothetical theology of Apostolic identity to our social media presence. Do we understand our lives to have enough value "just" as a child of God or do we busy ourselves trying to drum up enough of a life to get the ever-cherished "like" of a "friend"?

In addition to this confused sense of reality, social media distorts our engagement with community. I think of the irony represented by a picture I saw on Facebook recently of family members sitting in their living room on a holiday, each staring down at a phone. Such scenarios are typical of the way we spend time together. To ask a student-aged individual to turn her phone off to sit through a class or meeting is as foreign to her as if you asked her to cut off three fingers. Some studies suggest young people who have grown up with mobile devices actually experience physical symptoms of separation anxiety when separated from their phones. In fact, in January of 2015 the University of Missouri released the results of a study that found that phone users performed worse on tests when separated from their devices, indicating we consider our phones extensions of ourselves. It's not unreasonable to extrapolate that we are so dependent on our phones because of the sense of community and connectedness we think such devices provide.

If we are committed to embracing our royal identity, we should be seeking to mirror God to others. To do that, we've got to connect on a personal level. God was present among His people—so much so that He became flesh and came to earth to minister to us. He is still an ever-present God today (Psalm 46:1). And yet there is a growing inability in our world for people to be present. How often do we even look up from our screens to look at those talking to us? When is the last time you put your phone away—or even down—to carry on a conversation? For our image to reflect God's image, we've got to give ourselves to others and be present when we're with them. A couple of generations ago one of our songs celebrated that God was "never busy, always on the line."[5] The contemporary version of that song could just as easily celebrate that God never multitasks when you want to talk. He gives all of Himself to being present with us. Gray areas for interpretation, but if we want to mirror Him in who we are, we are called to a ministry of presence that focuses on, values, and celebrates fellow human beings by fully being with them.

In the middle of a myriad of social networking applications and sites popping up by the second, is it possible the proliferation of online social networking only devalues our relationships by giving us a false sense of connectedness? Does having fourteen hundred "friends" on a social site erode the power of that very word?

Joe Robinson, author of the book *Don't Miss Your Life*, wrote, "It's a little ironic that, as social media pushes the virtual friend count to new heights, the culture as a whole is getting ever more isolated. Researchers say that Americans have fewer close confidants outside family than ever before. One in four have no confidants at all."[6] As the number of our digital connections grow, our isolation does too as we spend that much less time away from actual face-to-face relationships.

Social media detracts from community by conveying a false sense of connectedness that is weak upon closer scrutiny. In a 2012 article in *The Atlantic*, Stephen Marche explained, "We meet fewer people. We gather less. And when we gather, our bonds are less meaningful and less easy. The decrease in confidants—that is, in quality social connections—has been dramatic over the past 25 years."[7] Because we think we have such a broad network of friends, we make less effort to engage in community in actuality. Additionally, with the convenience social media offers of managing "friends" on your own terms, Marche suggests many people are retreating from actual relationships for virtual friendships.

Let's be clear: I am not a fan of tossing your cell phone and computer in the backyard and living in a cave with no electricity. I concede that social media has its benefits. It's 657 miles from my driveway to where my handsome nephew and beautiful nieces live. I am thankful for convenient social media tools that enable me to see a picture of his first haircut and their angel costumes for the Christmas play. But I also realize that technology is no substitute for my getting on the floor with them to read a book together. By the same token, any efforts to build a sense of community from social media alone will face limitations. We need each other—not just projections of one another through a flat screen, but face-to-face, heart-to-heart interaction.

Scripture compares the church to a bride, a body, and a temple, and in each metaphor, there is a communal aspect. Just as we are all baptized into one body (I Corinthians 12:13), there is a relational factor to being God's people. We speak of the family of God, and if you've ever experienced loss or trouble and been comforted and helped by the church, you understand the familial language. But our relationships don't begin and end with our fellow church members. We are sent into a world that needs the hope we have (II Corinthians 5:18–19), and reaching them means touching lives of people beyond our normal social circle at church. Will social media distort the family nature of the church? Will social media help or hurt us in our efforts to build relationships with others outside our church?

Only time will provide conclusive answers. However, we should remain cautious of something that sociologists have established can erode community and foster isolation. We must set safeguards to ensure that our online activity does not become a substitute for genuine relationships and actual human contact. These safeguards may include setting time limits on our amount of social media consumption. Yet rather than merely creating a list of social media restrictions, perhaps we need to treat the root cause instead of just the symptoms. In this book we have argued that we are children of God who wear His name and that this revelation should shape how we live. In the light of social media, first our Apostolic identity should be clear. If there is a contradiction between who we project to our audience and who our closest friends know us to be, we should stop and have an honest self-evaluation. Second we must ask God to deliver us from any pressure we feel consciously or subconsciously to live a life that wins the approval of our social media followers.

With a commitment to staying true to our Apostolic identity online, we should also then turn back to being intentional in engaging in face-to-face community. There were reasons churches of yesterday had fellowship meetings, multi-night revivals, and dinner-on-the-ground. If our church culture no longer can fit those events in our schedules, we would be well served to look for new means of bringing the body together for community.

Environmental conservationists have learned the best way to combat erosion is to add or plant materials that give the eroding soil something to which it can cling—whether a hay bale staked to the side of a hill or used Christmas trees stacked along beaches to obstruct sand from being swept away. We can't stop the progress of technology and its eroding toll, but we can stake down some face-to-face measures of relationship-building around which we can nurture community.

QUESTIONS FOR REFLECTION

- Just as problem-laden as youthful oversharing in social media are the prideful attempts at image management we attempt in an effort to manipulate people's impressions of us. Have you ever engineered moments to try to look good in front of others?
- Have you ever found yourself manufacturing life experiences so you could have material to broadcast on social media?
- Do you find yourself frequently comparing yourself to others?
- Are your efforts to connect with and care for your friends and loved ones as intentional as your efforts to connect with your friends on social media?
- Whom did you spend the most time communicating with this week? Does this answer reflect the prioritization of the relationships you value?
- Compare the time you spent in social media with the time you spent in voluntary face-to-face communication; do you feel the time is out of proportion?

PRAYER

Lord Jesus, the identity You have given us as Your sons and daughters frees us from the pressure to impress those around us or prove our worth by their estimations. I thank You that I am who Your Word says I am. Father, please forgive me for times I have taken for granted or even despised the unique person You have created me to be. I repent of efforts to pridefully manage my image in a way that I think will win me points with others. I want to surrender my life to You and live only for Your approval and Your purposes. I vow to accept who You created me to be and reflect security in that identity in the way I live my life and how I present it on social media. In every area of my life, I want You to be glorified.

CHAPTER 18

WHEN GRASSHOPPERS ATTACK

People don't always get along. It's a sad reality to establish on the heels of how much we were designed to work together. The original grasshopper family was cursed by this flaw. Two brothers living different lives approached the Lord with sacrifices. One brother's offering was accepted and the other's was not. The Bible does not comment on Cain's motives, but his choice to murder his innocent brother must have involved the worst level of jealousy, revenge, and self-contempt. Of course the best scenario would have been for Cain to simply follow the principles God had established. Yet even in the face of his shortcomings, how could he have ever rationalized that killing his brother would in any way help his dilemma? That's the problem, you see. When a person's mind becomes bogged in an insecure, jealous grasshopper mentality, it distorts his ability to rationalize. A sane Cain who understood himself to be part of the first family with a wide-open future of possibility would have known that violence was not on the table. But grasshoppers don't think; they simply lash out at anyone who by their successes make the other grasshoppers feel smaller.

You can see it with King Saul. He was king! What could he have possibly wished for? But insecure grasshoppers are never satisfied, and enough is never enough. Because they are not secure in themselves, their minds are plagued with jealousies and vengefulness that leads to the most unthinkable acts. And so a grasshopper king who had all of the possibilities of a great future with the favor and blessings of being handpicked by God (I Samuel 10:6–7) became consumed by jealousy when God used David to slay Goliath (I Samuel 18:6–8). The grasshopper king's demise was death on a battlefield with his family instead of mentoring his protégé so the kingdom could expand triumphantly.

Grasshopper jealousy has less to do with those around us and everything to do with ourselves. Lewis and Demarest explain,

> Our view of the worth of others may be low because of a low view of ourselves. Men and women who affirm the reality and dignity of God's image-bearers universally ought to see the implications of that truth for their own *self-image*. We ought to cease considering ourselves naked apes or meat machines. We are not mere victims of class interests, economic aggrandizement, genetic programming, cultural conditioning, or historical necessity. Like other persons, we ourselves have inestimable worth as self-transcendent subjects and moral agents. Our inherent value cannot be taken away by any mistake or failure. Because of what we *are* spiritually

and physically, our lives are of greater value than
any impersonal project in the whole world.[1]

As children of God made in His image, we should be secure
in that identity and likewise appreciate our brothers and sisters.
That perspective has no room for jealousies, competition, and
attacking.

But in addition to the innate humanness we grapple with, we
live in an increasingly complicated world. Scholar and psychologist Kenneth Gergen put it this way, "As we absorb the views,
values, and visions of others, and live out the multiple plots in
which we are enmeshed, we enter a postmodern consciousness. It
is a world in which we no longer experience a secure sense of self,
and in which doubt is increasingly placed on the very assumption
of a bounded identity with palpable attributes."[2] Because of the
myriad of voices in our society each declaring its own merit and
superiority, many people get lost in the endless barrage, either
competing for approval or vying against the frontrunners amid the
ever-changing values and trends our world hurtles at us. It would
be nice if simply knowing that God built us to be relational beings
designed to work together in communities resolved all the petti-
ness that often troubles otherwise good people. But the headlines
tell a different story.

We need to deal with the consequences of jealousy and competition, but let's first examine the root problem. Without getting into the
nature versus nurture debate, let us say that a number of influences shape our personal sense of identity. Unfortunately that shapes
our outlook on others. The person trapped in a grasshopper mentality can't be happy for others or see their goodness and gifts, so
consumed is the grasshopper in coping with her own seeming insufficiencies. Have you ever met someone who constantly complains?

Nothing is ever good enough at the house or the job or the church. Is it because the person is not happy with himself?

I have a friend who teaches the teen Sunday school class. Talk about wading through the waters of insecurity and identity crises. This teacher's unswerving mission is to embed in the class a commitment to live for an audience of One. She's passionate about it the way I am about campaigning to get the McRib on the permanent menu because she's convinced there aren't enough atta-boys, carrots, sticks, or any other teaching mechanism that will short-circuit unhealthy behavior motivated by a desire to secure the attention or validation of others. Only a commitment from students to live with eyes locked on Jesus alone can direct healthy choices for an overcoming life.

I think she's on to something. I wish I could tell you that at thirty-never-you-mind I have embedded that mantra in my life as well. Instead I must confess to occasional petty worries about impressing friends and family to feel secure in who I am. That is problematic for a number of reasons. First, it discounts the ultimate innate value I have as a child of God. Second, when I resort to those motives for establishing my worth, I am driven by a deep-rooted hunger for acceptance that negotiates and compromises, permitting unacceptable choices and actions. With those ungodly jealousies raging, I can justify and rationalize behaviors that hurt others and myself in a quest for attention and acceptance.

Paul put it all in perspective when he wrote his first letter to the Corinthians with a voice of correction. In Paul's estimation, God didn't pick the Corinthians based on their wisdom, power, and social status. Paul even argued that God picked the most unlikely things to use so He would get the glory (I Corinthians 1:26–31). That might explain why Moses with his speaking insecurities, Rahab with a haunted past, and Peter with so many self-control problems would be part of God's grand epic. We can't look back at those scenarios and give all the credit to the individuals; rather we see the grace of God at work in their lives and have hope for God to perform His promises in our own stories.

When my identity and validation comes not from others patting me on the back but from being confident in God's love for me and in pursuing His purpose, I'm not jealous of others. I don't have to compete with anyone for attention or affection. I can joyfully accept my place in the Kingdom and rejoice at others' favor and blessings.

I believe God gets frustrated and downright angry about any jealousies, competitions, or other sources that disrupt unity because they keep the church from working together to fulfill the vision and purpose God has for us: the desperate work of taking the love of God we have experienced to the rest of the hurting, broken world. To follow Paul's writings in I Corinthians, we see that in chapter 3 he went on to explain that some plant and some water to illustrate the necessity of the church working together with God ultimately giving the increase. He reminded the Corinthians that there was no room for pride in that purpose—only unity to see God at work (I Corinthians 3:4–9).

Competition in our world is so ingrained it consumes us. In moments when we shake ourselves and discover its hold for what it is, it can be frightening. Peer pressure may seem a passé concept, but oh how relevant it still is.

In 2015, a young adult shared a social media post that tells the tale:

> Hello, my name is ----, and I am an addict. I wake up and the 1st thing I do is open my phone to check Instagram and Facebook. It's like I have this unquenched desire that I need to "catch

up" and make sure I didn't miss someone's post throughout the night. It's like I can't get my phone opened fast enough. I hate this feeling. Throughout my day- I have to take breaks to get "caught up." To see what 'he' or 'she' is doing today. I have this emptiness inside of me that is not filled until I have successfully scrolled through my Instagram account and looked at every post until I meet up to the picture that I stopped on the last time. It's an addiction. I am addicted. It controls my mind. It consumes my day. It leaves me depressed and feeling non-content with my life. If you know me personally, then you know that I am a very happy person. I am happy and joyful in every aspect of my life until I get on social media and immediately start to question the excitement of my life because suddenly I want what 'they' have, or I want to go where they are going. This, my friends is no less addicting than a person hooked on drugs or alcohol. For this reason, I am taking the first step and admitting my addiction. Next I am stepping away from the public scene for awhile to re-discover and fine-tune my happiness and contentment within myself. I'm sure none of my friends struggle with this, but I have for a long time- and it is time to address it. I want to impact people with my words and my lifestyle. I want my life to be clear from distractions so The Almighty can do with me what He wishes. I am entering into a quiet season- and I couldn't be more excited. Hello, my name is ---- I am addicted to social media, BUT I am on the road to recovery. [Posted 5/13/15]

We've already studied the dangers of technology and social media. Now look beyond the medium itself to deeper issues. Notice words like "non-content" and "emptiness." The word the post didn't include was "competition" but can you hear it? Social media has given us a platform to dive headlong into an all-out competition for who has the best life. When we compete, many people have to give themselves to the contest in all-consuming ways, and someone has to lose.

As thought-provoking to me as the post were the comments:

> Comment#1: Such a great post and such an example to girls younger than you!!

> Comment#2: I just adore you. You're such a beautiful person and such a wonderful role model!

> Comment#3: Wow! Girl I feel the same way!! I think if we all admitted it you would be shocked at how many of us are feeling the same. Thanks for being open.

> Comment#4: You just put my thoughts into words!! I've been thinking this lately too! That I need to fast social media and spend more time on my relationship with God and my daughter! Once I fast it, it always comes easier to slowly weaning myself off to not getting on as much ☺ I love you and your beautiful soul!

> Comment#5: I am so proud of you for posting this. Love you!

I hear in these comments a trend—voices joining to acknowledge this soul quest to overcome the consuming competition to keep up with others.

This obsession with broadcasting ourselves and competing for attention is no new thing. In the mid-1960s, my grandmother developed a program at the Louisiana School for the Deaf in which parents of preschoolers sent in illustrated reports of life at home each morning. She discovered an interesting trend exemplified in one student:

> All went well with one parent while the child was three, but during her fourth year she began dis-carding the paper Mama had prepared in favor of more recent happenings. For example, if Mama boiled cray-fish one afternoon, Chantelle was very happy with an illustrated sentence. If friends came over later, Chantelle would shake her head sadly at the mother as she threw the paper in the trash, and would indicate with fresh paper and a pen that Mama must write a new sentence. Sometimes the second paper would be dis-carded because Chantelle had seen something interesting on the way to school.[3]

Always craving the latest, greatest, most [fill-in-the-blank], our carnal grasshopper appetites to compete with others for best life and best experiences are insatiable.

The only cure for this competition between grasshoppers is to turn our eyes from one another for validation and look to the giver of life. Oh, I'm not suggesting we can ever be cured from compe-tition. The smallest children will race for who can get to the water fountain first, and the oldest men in domino tournaments will fight for the title. But these competitions can be put in perspective in a way that does not consume our lives.

We need to understand that loving Him involves loving others. He said those commandments were inseparable (Matthew 22:36–40). Ever noticed how a parent can be at about 6.2 on the 1–10 scale when her child is fighting with a toy, pet, or even the parent, but let the child turn his anger on a sibling. Anger shoots off the charts. Sibling fights seem to frustrate parents like nothing else. Is it possible God gets more frustrated when we can't get along with each other? On the other hand, imagine His joy when we operate from a place of unity and love. It's liberating as one author discovered:

> Renouncing my old value system—in which I had to compete with other people on the basis of power, wealth, and talent—and committing myself to Christ, the Head, abruptly frees me. My sense of competition fades. No longer do I have to bristle against life, seizing ways to prove myself. In my new identity my ideal has become to live my life in such a way that people around me recognize Jesus and His love, not my own set of distinctive qualities. My worth and acceptance are enveloped in Him.[4]

Finally, what do we do when others attack us? We pray. Lewis and Demarest argue, "Our political, social, ecclesiastical, and other opponents have inherent worth as persons. Because they are image-bearers of the Creator we should show them respect and love. Insofar as it is in their power to do so Christians will pray for those who oppose them because of their faith, and they will do so just as Christ prayed from the cross, 'Father forgive them, for they do not know what they are doing' (Luke 23:34)."[5]

QUESTIONS FOR REFLECTION

- In what areas of your life do you struggle with feelings of insecurity?
- How do your own insecurities affect the way you treat others around you?
- Is it possible you have fallen into jealousy, envy, and competition with others that detracts from the unity God envisions for His people?
- How can you commit to a new future?

PRAYER

Father, because You call me Your child, I can take confidence in who you have made me to be. I confess there have been times when I have let my frustrations and insecurities with myself affect the way I have viewed and treated others. Heal me of those wounds and help me to see myself as complete in You. Help me to use that understanding to treat others with dignity and compassion as Your beloved children.

CHAPTER 19

GRASSHOPPERS ENCOURAGING OTHER GRASSHOPPERS

One of Louisiana's treasured fiction writers of recent years, Tim Gautreaux, titled one of his books *Welding with Children*. I always grinned when my fellow students spoke with awe about the book as though the title were somehow outlandish or especially imaginative. To me it was the most plausible thing in the world. When Joel and I were seven and nine respectively, our grandfather taught us to weld. Well, maybe not weld, but cut. As usual, we were spending Friday night with our grandparents, and shortly before dark, we were out behind the house with our grandfather, watching him work.

My grandfather was working on one of his custom-built trailers as I recall. By "custom-built" I mean he'd detached the bed of a pickup truck and by means that escape the limits of my engineering knowledge, attached a tongue to the truckbed, thereby resulting in a trailer. Seeing no reason for us to look on in the process without helping out, my grandfather scrounged up gloves and slapped the welding hood on Joel. (Our family believed in the 4-H "learning by doing" motto.) Granddaddy did a commendable job of demonstrating how to cut with the torch, and we were cutting a massive plate of sheet metal as instructed with great aplomb until my grandmother noticed the quiet house and decided to investigate.

I don't remember all the details, but our welding careers didn't proceed much further past that afternoon. What I do remember is the complete (and possibly ludicrous) degree of confidence my grandfather had in us. My grandmother had a matching gift for lauding our academic abilities and general wonderfulness. Every child should have a family who believes in them with wild abandon. It is more than a heady, feet-don't-touch-the-ground nonsense, but a genuine understanding of unlimited potential spread wide before a child.

Social scientists would tell us that the parental opinion of a child shapes his or her sense of identity and worth. "Several studies have been reported which indicate that parents exert a powerful influence on the formation of a child's self-concept (Fitts, 1971). . . . One widely accepted theory pertaining to the development of the self is that a child's self-evaluation is profoundly influenced by 'significant' persons, particularly his parents. . . . As a child is appraised by 'significant others,' so he in time appraises himself (Jersild, 1968: 172)."[1] How wonderful and yet terrifying. Parents, you have an enormous amount of power to influence your children. You form the foundation of their identity and their sense of worth. (See the parental sections of James E. Hightower Jr.'s *Caring for People from Birth to Death* for helpful directives.[2])

I hate that I have to admit this statement, but it's true: the grasshopper effect is contagious. In fact, perhaps we should have called it the grasshopper syndrome since families and friends pass down identity, unfortunately with insecurities carrying more weight than confidence. Intimidated, scared, underprivileged mentalities spread like wildfire. I've often wondered why it's so much harder to excite people about something positive than it is to bring people down with something negative. I still don't know why that is, but it's a truth about human beings from the earliest of times.

Once more let's revisit our grasshoppers at the threshold of the Promised Land. When Moses reflected back on the unraveling of epic proportions on a day that should have been marked in Jewish history as one of the greatest military conquests of all time, the great patriarch delivered a woeful lament: "You complained in your tents, and said, 'Because the Lord hates us, He has brought us out of the land of Egypt to deliver us into the hand of the Amorites, to destroy us. Where can we go up? Our brethren have discouraged our hearts'" (Deuteronomy 1:27–28). When analyzing the fallout in hindsight, Moses identified the power of negative persuasion: the spies discouraged an entire people. Ten intimidated men locked in a mental prison of unrealized identity swayed an entire nation of over a million people and blocked a promise generations in the making. That—as terrifying as it is— shows the power of grasshoppers. The very men who thought they were not powerful enough to defeat an army of Amorites in turn shut down God's army with only their words. They were not tiny, incompetent grasshoppers; they were something much more fierce—a powerful SEAL team of grasshoppers who, with their discouragement, blocked the people of God's ability to have faith and take action to receive their promises and royal inheritances.

I shudder at the thought of the possibility that with a negative word here, a hopeless shrug there, or any lack of encouragement to a brother or sister, I may have blocked a dream or a promise from God that He had whispered to them. But rather than getting stuck in the debilitating thoughts of what might have been, I resolve to take action in a positive direction. Going forward I will look for ways to encourage others to embrace the identity God has designed for us. I can be a Joshua or Caleb, and you can too.

We need Joshuas who will put a stop to negative thinking. With you alone lies the choice and the power to put an end to the spread of criticism about your church, your family, your brothers and sisters. You can stop the negativity with your silence and refusal to pass on the virus. You also have the choice to take the offensive and spread positive words.

This role of encouraging other grasshoppers often is most effective when we reach out to our circle of influence: those in our care or those slightly younger than us. Whether we realize it or not, other eyes are on us. That knowledge should not make us paranoid, but it should prompt a sense of responsibility. Given our previous claim that we are baptized into the body of Christ to reach out to one another, we should be committed to caring for those around us.

With permission I have borrowed this helpful piece on mentoring from a pastoral standpoint. I concede that this material was crafted with a church leader in mind, but everyone in the body of Christ is called to care for others. I challenge you to substitute the word "Christian" for "pastor" in the passage below and see if you hear the call to help, to mentor, and to encourage those a few years behind you in this life journey:

> Before we say that this generation is weird, different, unreachable, and unable to be understood, we must realize that the way Jesus led is the same way today's pastors must lead. He gathered a group that desired to be mentored and took them just about everywhere He went. They

watched Him pray and thus learned how to pray. They watched Him heal and cast out devils, thus they learned what it took to heal the sick and cast out devils. In only three and one half years, the men He led were equipped with the tools they needed to change the world. After the Holy Ghost filled their lives, that power jump-started the things they had learned from the Lord. What they had learned by watching Jesus and being with Jesus gave them the ability to start churches, direct world-wide mission programs, train lay leaders in the church and establish the framework for world-wide revival.

Many people would label this generation as a band of misfits, with strange ideas, and who simply want to push the limits. Look at the crew Jesus assembled on His team. There were bold ones, like Peter, who simply needed some direction and someone to really believe in him. There were deep, passionate ones, like John, who were just looking for someone to let them get close to Him. There were the doubters, like Thomas, who just need a little extra attention.

God has placed in your church a unique, gifted, diverse generation who needs the proper guidance, direction, and training so that their special and diverse gifts can impact the world, preparing it for the soon return of the Lord. . . . The approachable and collaborative pastor will successfully lead this next generation and help them become all they were meant to be.³

We can influence our generation. We must. A revelation of who we are as children of God includes a revelation that we were built for relationships with one another and designed to work together in the body of Christ. Your gifts weren't given for you to enjoy in a vacuum. We were created to live interconnectedly and to help one another.

Encouraging others must begin with the conviction that all people are made in the image of God and as such have inherent worth and should be treated with dignity. Lewis and Demarest reiterate this book's premise:

> Because humans are real spiritual beings who will relate to God forever in loving fellowship or will be alienated from God, each person is of inestimable temporal and eternal value and significance. Persons have this inward worth inalienably as creatures of God made in the image of God. Their value goes far beyond that of their amazing bodies or that of being the highest animal on earth. Their value is not diminished when for some reason and for some time they are not useful to society in the form of their family, church, or nation. Every living human being is of intrinsic worth—poor or rich, female or male, educated or not, lighter or darker—because he or she is an endlessly existing active spiritual person like God.⁴

Every one of our brothers and sisters are special to God and therefore should be special to us. Next we must believe that God can work through us to minister to our brothers and sisters. J. Mark

Jordan advises, "God has gifted each of us with a special ministry that He wants us to use in service to Him. . . . Opportunities will present themselves to you in many ways. The richest and most fulfilling days are ahead of you when you see other people respond to your spiritual influence."[5]

With a belief that all people have worth, we simply commit to affirming their identity and worth. Consequently, we cannot be afraid of affirming words. Maybe we worried in times past that glowing remarks would puff people up with pride they couldn't handle. No one wants to feed that monster. But if we have the right identity, which includes a humility from understanding God is the author and giver of the good things in our lives, pride is nullified because all credit is turned over to God. Meanwhile, the encouraging words we are bottling up could be keeping others from building their understanding of what God wants to do with their lives. What would be wrong with offering these statements to those around us who bless us: "I am so thankful for what God is doing in your life. I am so thankful God used you to minister to us today. God has blessed you with gifts, and I appreciate your using them for His kingdom."

David and Nancy Norris are pioneers in this area with a profound understanding of the power of the gift of encouragement and mentoring. I saved one of their emails and keep it always. At the risk of being misunderstood as self-congratulatory, I'm going to share a portion of their email because it reveals a key to their understanding for the need to encourage: "Ministry is never easy, and the will of God is pretty tricky, particularly when you are on a trail that has never been blazed before; if you can count on one hand the people who rightly appreciate what you are doing and why, you are rich." I am rich because I consider David and Nancy Norris as two such people on that one hand. And I am doubly rich because I have enough people to fill a second hand as well. I am sad at the realization that there are probably many others who can't say the same. Perhaps you are one of them. Let me assure you that Jesus will never leave you in your journey to do His work. And let me go a step further and encourage you that He will use His body and send someone in your path to show you appreciation and support in those challenging moments and seasons. In the meantime, find a way to pour into someone else's life. Encouragement has a beautiful way of doubling back.

My grandfather's last words to me were "I'm proud of you." I don't know why, but that made a difference. I can also remember a place in the hallway of my home church where my pastor's wife spoke a word of affirmation about my future. And I can tell you how my pastor commending me on my work affected me in such a deep and unexpected way. He validated something I didn't know needed validating.

We are made in God's image, so is it any wonder that just as God loves and uplifts us in near, personal ways we are called to love and affirm others in our lives? One physician studying human nature spoke of the way we give that help: "We want psychological formulas as precise as those techniques I study in my surgery manuals. But the human psyche is too complex for a manual. The best we can offer is to be there, to see and to touch. . . . Taken together, these provide a sense of presence to the world—God's presence."[6] I can't give you a script of the right words to say. However, by our presence, our kindness, and our genuine appreciation of others, we can help our brothers and sisters rise above the grasshopper effect of misplaced identity and become who God calls them to be.

QUESTIONS FOR REFLECTION

- Have there been times you have yielded to negativity when you could have been more positive and supportive? How can you amend this?
- Who around you could you be encouraging?
- What are ways you can encourage and support them?

PRAYER

Jesus, I thank You for times in my life where You brought someone alongside me to encourage me in dark seasons. I thank You for the gifts You have placed in the body of Christ and how my brothers and sisters have used the gift of language to build me up and encourage me in special times. I want to do that for others. I ask You to give me a sensitivity to Your direction on how I can be an encouragement. Help me to point others to You for a vision of Your purpose and Your calling. Thank You that You love us and we always find hope and encouragement in Your presence.

CHAPTER 20

GRASSHOPPERS UNDER FIRE

We grew up in a small town in Louisiana called Walker. It was so small that when Sonic built a franchise in our town when I was in the fifth grade, all of the community flocked to see the sight, effectively shutting down the town. Then McDonald's came to town when I was a freshman in high school, and that really got our attention. People took off work, skipped school, and got out of other responsibilities to be there for the grand opening. All the cool kids at the high school decided to go to McDonald's for breakfast before school, so the Walker Police had to come out to direct traffic. Our world had expanded, and we were sure that was as good as life could get.

Now I don't want to embellish the story too much. Baton Rouge was twenty-three miles west of us and growing, so we could go to town and experience nice things. But in some very real senses, our world was small.

My last year of high school one of our French teachers decided to take the French club to Paris, Monaco, and Barcelona. Now a few among the group had gotten off a cruise ship in another country. Some of us had traveled to neighboring Texas and walked across the border to Mexico for a few moments. But by and large we'd not left the States.

From this context, our brave French teacher took us across the pond to see the world. And it was special. We saw the lavishness of Monaco, the phenomenal architecture of Barcelona, the lovely countryside of France, the famous Notre Dame, and the epic la tour Eiffel. We even got a full tour of le Louvre, where some of the most famous works of art in the world are showcased, as well as the equally famous palace of Versailles that Louis XIV built, which was the most fascinating thing I'd ever seen.

And yet eleven days later when our plane touched down in New Orleans, in the eyes of a group of eighteen year olds, that lavish world we left couldn't compare to home. It was before the days of airport security as we now know it. Parents and family members clustered around the gate, waiting for us. When our feet stepped off that plane and across the sliver of space that separated us from the airport, that muggy June New Orleans air wafted through and we caught the smell of home. I don't know who started it or if it was instinctive in us all, but what I know is we ran up that cattle chute of a gate and breathlessly bounded into the arms of our parents. We were home and we were glad.

The most magnificent castle or palace of this world cannot compare with home. Yes, we celebrate the handiwork of God in this world and do not denigrate His creation, but this is not our permanent home. I have caught the aroma of a place I know I belong. I am running toward the Gate. I am a redeemed grasshopper on my way home.

Understanding who we are means understanding we are a people in a state of transition. Some suggest our sense of identity comes from our sense of place.[1] One of the go-to questions when we meet someone is "Where are you from?" Placing them somewhere physically in the world helps us understand their identity. What does it mean about our identity when we're from a place not in this world? What kind of identity do you have when you are a temporary resident?

It means the achievements of this world pale in comparison to the eternal things we can achieve. Jesus taught in the famous message on the mountain: "Do not lay up for yourselves treasures on earth, where moth and rust destroy and where thieves break in and steal; but lay up for yourselves treasures in heaven, where neither moth nor rust destroys and where thieves do not break in and steal. For where your treasure is, there your heart will be also" (Matthew 6:19–21).

The rest of the story is that since this world is not our home, we cannot be surprised or overwhelmed when difficulties face us in this temporary place. Jesus even said, "In the world you will have tribulation; but be of good cheer, I have overcome the world" (John 16:33). Trials are the reality, but Jesus is the hope.

With an understanding of who we are and the charge to use your Apostolic identity to minister to others, you're almost invincible, aren't you! Almost. It would be nice if knowledge alone shaped us. But God seems to believe in the 4-H motto of learning by doing. It seems much of what we learn in our Christian living comes through experience.

Perhaps that's why Peter and James spoke pretty plainly in their letters about the reality that difficult experiences will come. One of the most difficult things as a preacher of the gospel is ministering to large crowds when you know the needs cover such a sweeping range. Of course we know the Holy Ghost has a way of ministering to each individual on a personal level, but it's always tough to give an altar call when you know the word of faith or conviction you've preached applies differently to people with disparate circumstances. The conclusion of this book is one of those moments.

Some of you reading this book have made mistakes of your own accord and you are living with consequences of your own choices and volition. You may struggle with anger directed toward yourself and frustrations over years lost because of your own choices. You need to know Jesus loves you, and you need to receive His grace and show it to yourself in moments of frustration.

Does it mean God has given up on you or there is something fundamentally wrong with you if you face struggles, addiction, or persistent temptation? No, no, no. It means you are still breathing. If we were perfect, it would mean we do not need God. Instead, God created us with a free will so we could make the choice to follow Him: "As humans we are not prisoners of our bodies, nor of our own past habits or conditioning, for we have a reflexive ability to criticize ourselves and by God's universal or special grace to change some of our fundamental patterns of thought."[2] The gift to reflect on your life and your past is a means to choose God's grace to make changes, but it is not a license to condemn yourself. You are human. You will make mistakes. You change, grow, and move on. Don't compound the past by refusing to surrender it to God; accept His grace, forgiveness, and new identity for you.

Jesus picked twelve grasshoppers to be His posse. Think of the twelve He chose to remain closest to Him. Sure there was the physician, but there were fishermen, a despised tax collector, a guy who struggled with His temper and his faith level, and one who was greedy. The group even included a betrayer and a denier with the only difference being one disciple's willingness to choose repentance and change. What a motley crew.

Author David Orton reminds us, "Jesus seeks out and saves the ridiculously small, the despised, the insignificant and the lost, and he takes the part of the little ones that follow the shepherd and bravely go out on his mission. In this he echoes Yahweh's championing and heroicization of the disadvantaged and despised, those whose perception and recognition of their smallness moves them to rely on his rescue and empowerment, in line with his covenant commitment. This little one, who feels like a grasshopper in present company, may take comfort in that."[3] No one ever has to feel worthless in God's kingdom. The flaws of the original disciples along with the number of people who have found new identities in Jesus speaks volumes about the kind of disciples Jesus is still looking for today.

Still others of you are reading this book and while you're not claiming to be perfect, the difficulties you've faced in your past or perhaps are facing now are outside of your control. Other people, and perhaps the faceless phenomenon that is life itself, have put in your path obstacles that seem impossible or overwhelming at best.

May I put this into final perspective? If we believe any part of Scripture, we have to believe God loves us. I know this book has already covered this and it may feel like an overstatement, but the way we live and speak of ourselves often betrays a core belief about God's love for us. We can believe He loves others, but we often fail to believe He accepts, loves, and is committed to caring for us personally for the long haul. If being loved by God is not enough for you, nothing else ever will be. Your personal goals, your family, your friends—not only will they in time fail you, but even in the most perfect scenarios, they will not be enough. God's love is the only constant you can count on, and the only source that can root your identity in something filling and lasting. If you're still struggling with accepting that truth, which I know can be easier said than done, stop here and go back and read chapter four over and over as many times as it takes to come to peace with the reality that Jesus loves you.

Now if you are firmly convinced that God loves you, then let me call you to believe the next step: when situations and events happen in life, those events do not affect God's love for us. In other words, if I believe God loves me, if I receive a cancer diagnosis, it is not because God stopped loving me. At the same time, if I am blessed with a great promotion at my job, it is not because God loves me a little extra this month. God loves me because He created me for His good pleasure and wired into who He is is an unconditional love for me that can't be diminished or propped up or altered by the specific things I do or do not do.

From that backdrop then, I can read Peter and James's advice about trials as a reality of coping with life. Many good devout Christians get hung up here; you might even say these theodicy questions, or questions about God's justice and our response to suffering, form the ultimate question of apologetics (the defense of Christianity). Some theologians would argue that God is at work aligning a million minute details of our day at all times. Others would see God as a cosmic watchmaker who winds up the great mechanism of time and chance, turns us all loose, and sits back to watch with folded arms impervious to the chaos that ensues. Is it possible God is somewhere in the middle?

Though this book does not pretend to take on such a massive topic definitively, let me taking a passing swipe. We've shared with you about a God who handcrafted us. He even went so far as to die for us to buy us back from a penalty of sin that would have separated us from Him for eternity. If I can get my head around that, then I can begin to trust that He will be with me when I go through tough times. I can even understand Romans to mean that while not everything is good that happens to me, God will work everything out in a way that the end result can still be good (Romans 8:28).

The twelve spies' story revealed a God with a plan for His people to be prosperous conquerors. He still wants His people to be triumphant today. You'll notice, however, that even with the twelve spies, God did not open the earth and swallow the inhabitants of the Promised Land nor send a scourge of sickness to wipe them out. He gave His children the opportunity and the free will to claim the promise if they chose to step out in faith to operate in the mission and in the giftings God had for them.

Today God still gives us opportunities and promises. But it's up to us to trust God to be with us and to step out in faith. Those opportunities are not without challenges. We will face giants as we are on the path to promise. In those moments, we must take God at His Word, believe we are who He has said we are, and stay committed to the purpose He has called us to embrace. We have His promise for triumph: "Through God we will do valiantly, For it is He who shall tread down our enemies" (Psalm 108:13).

It's all a matter of perspective. A redeemed grasshopper surrendered to God and united with others can't be stopped. Look at the men who resisted the grasshopper mentality of their fellow spies. Joshua took the reins after Moses and led the children of Israel into the Promised Land. Caleb asked Joshua for his mountain God promised, went to battle at eighty-five years old, and ran the enemy out to take the land (Joshua 14:6–14; Judges 1:20). A child of God with a promise never quits.

Not quitting doesn't mean there won't be setbacks. T. F. Tenney recounts the story of how Israel went back to calling himself Jacob after his sons murdered Hamor and Shechem and crisis ensued (Genesis 34); yet God visited Israel and reminded him of his rightful name: "You get your identity from your altars. . . . Jacob almost gave up on himself because of a family crisis; God did not give up on him. God called him by name. . . . We cannot be defined by names given to us by anyone other than God. The enemy cannot be allowed to haunt and taunt us about whom and what we used to be. God is ever present to remind us of who we are in Him. We must remember that God recognizes who we truly are."[4]

I wish I could promise you that the end result would be caviar on every plate and a Cadillac in every garage. But His kingdom is not of this world. He calls us to a purpose and gifts that have an otherworldly value. We are building up a crown that moths and dust can't touch. So keep believing, keep working, keep listening to His whisper, and keep ministering to others. One day you'll wear a crown not for a grasshopper but for a royal heir.

QUESTIONS FOR REFLECTION

- What is the biggest area of struggle in your life?
- How can you pray for God's help in this situation?
- As a concluding reflection, write out your understanding of your identity.
- Write your personal mission statement.
- Are there any final areas of your life (values, thought patterns, speech, habits) that need to change to more closely align you with your God-given identity and mission?

PRAYER

Father, I thank You for who You have called me to be. I know Your Word does not exempt me from struggle or even suffering, but it does assure me You will be with me. Thank You for that hope that You will never leave me nor forsake me. I ask for Your continued grace and strength to live out my God-given identity. In Jesus' name, amen.

AFTERWORD

On August 31, 2015, actress Julia Roberts released a social media post that the world found fascinating. Accompanied by a picture of herself without makeup, the Hollywood superstar—dare we say idol—offered this indictment:

> Perfect is a disease of a nation. We overlay our faces with tons of make-up. We get botoxs and even starve ourselves to become that perfect size. We try to fix something but you can't fix what you can't see. It's the soul that needs the surgery. It's time that we take a stand. How can you expect someone else to love you if you don't love yourself? You have to be happy with yourself. It doesn't matter what you look like on the outside, it's whats on the inside that counts. Today, I want to put up a makeup-free photo. I know I have wrinkles on my skin but today I want you to see beyond that. I want to embrace the real me and I want you to embrace who you are, the way you are, and love yourself just the way you are. [sic][1]

While I cautiously debated using a Hollywood actress's remarks to make a point founded on biblical principle, I hope to do something more here. I hope her comments show the reality of something humans fight universally: the social pressure we give into that leads to self-loathing and then gives way to destruction of ourselves. Even the editorial [sic] mark I used to indicate the grammar mistakes in the quote were the author's and not my own suggests this human tendency to critique and shift blame and find ways to deal with the pressure of inadequacy.

Ms. Roberts is correct on this point: it *is* the soul that needs surgery. Yet even in correctly diagnosing the problem, her treatment plan reveals what our world has overlooked. We don't solve a soul problem ourselves. We can't embrace ourselves or love ourselves enough to fix the condition. The fundamental answer our world must hear is that Jesus alone is the soul surgeon. Once we accept *His* love for us, He can perform that soul surgery, correct that brokenness inside that obsesses over imperfections, and give us peace within ourselves that comes from understanding our identity as a beloved child of God.

Through this book I hope you have been encouraged to turn any insecure or misdirected notions of identity you have over to a loving God who handcrafted you. I pray that you will put your soul in His capable hands so He can transform you into an overcomer, more than a conqueror, the head and not the tail. With the gifts, dreams, and purposes He will breathe into your life, you will be empowered to venture boldly forth into a land of promise—not a paradise of milk and honey, but a broken world of broken people Ms. Roberts describes who can be transformed by the message of the Cross and the hope that the God who loves you also loves them: "He is asking us to be the chief bearers of His likeness in the world. As spirit, He remains invisible on this planet. He relies on us to give flesh to that spirit, to bear the image of God."[2]

God will use you in unity with your brothers and sisters to bring His hope, His love, and His grace to a world of wounded grasshoppers still struggling to see beyond the giants of addiction, self-hate, and hopelessness. So you see, we are not really grasshoppers at all. We're regal priests and priestesses temporarily working for our Father the King until He calls us and all of the grasshoppers we've reached home to live out our royal identity for eternity.

NOTES

CHAPTER 1 INTRODUCTION

1. T. F. Tenney, "The Greatest Challenge of the Twenty-First Century," *IBC Perspectives* 26, no. 3 (March 2016): 20.

CHAPTER 2 THE ANATOMY OF GRASSHOPPERS

1. Berel Dov Lerner, "Timid Grasshoppers and Fierce Locusts: An Ironic Pair of Biblical Metaphors," *Vetus Testamentum* 49, no. 4:548.

2. Robert E. Morosco, "Theological Implications of Fear: The Grasshopper Complex." *Journal of Psychology & Theology* 1, no. 2 (April 1973): 47–48.

CHAPTER 3 GRASSHOPPERS INDEED

1. Kyle Idleman, *Gods at War: Defeating the Idols That Battle for Your Heart* (Grand Rapids, MI: Zondervan, 2013), 230–31.

2. Ibid., page 186.

CHAPTER 4 GOD LOVES GRASSHOPPERS

1. Mitchell Bland, "Worth It," Sermon at The Sanctuary UPC, Hazelwood, MO. http://www.thesanctuaryupc.com/pages/page.asp?page_id=296303&programId=241719. March 13, 2016.

CHAPTER 5 HANDMADE GRASSHOPPERS

1. Our identity as children of God is based on the belief that God made humans and all of creation (John 1:3; Colossians 1:16). For a defense of creationism, see David Gray's "Humanity" chapter of *Doctrines of the Bible* (Eds. J. L. Hall and David K. Bernard. Hazelwood, MO: Word Aflame Press, 1993) and Arlo Moehlenpah's *Creation Versus Evolution* (Hazelwood, MO: Word Aflame Press, 1998).

2. Robert Peterson and Covenant Theological Seminary, "Humanity, Christ, and Redemption," Lecture 2, page 4, https://www.covenantseminary.edu/resources/wpcontent/uploads/sites/5/2014/12/ST220_T_02.pdf.

3. Paul Brand and Philip Yancey, *In His Image* (Grand Rapids, MI: Zondervan, 1984) 22.

4. Ibid., page 5.

5. I include the following footnote from Gossard's paper: "The flip side of this is then the question of the meaning of Ps 51:5, 'I was shapen in iniquity.' Whether this refers to a collective sin of 'fallen' humanity after the expulsion from Eden, an individual and personal sense of intense guilt is beyond the scope of this study."

6. Everett Gossard, "What Is Man?" (Essay for Systematic Theology I Course, Urshan Graduate School of Theology, 2004), 4–5.

7. Brand and Yancey offer one of the most succinct surveys of the development of image of God theology: "Philosophers and theologians have long speculated on all that could be contained within the mystery of that single phrase. Predictably, they tend to project onto their definitions the principal concerns of their own era. The Enlightenment age assures us the image of God is the ability to reason, the Pietists identify it as the spiritual faculty, the Victorians claim it as the capacity to make moral judgments, and the Renaissance thinkers locate the image of God in artistic creativity. As for our own psychology-dominated age? What else could that image be, we are now advised, than our capacity for relationships with other people and with God." See Brand and Yancey's *In His Image*, 20.

8. David K. Bernard, Chapel Service Message, World Evangelism Center, June 17, 2015.

9. "In God's Image," Word Aflame Curriculum (Hazelwood, MO: Pentecostal Publishing House, Fall 2010, Lesson 3) 25.

10. Bud Chambers, "Born to Serve the Lord," Jimmie Davis Music, 1959.

11. Gordon R. Lewis and Bruce A. Demarest, *Integrative Theology* (Grand Rapids, MI: Zondervan, 1996) 174.

12. Jennifer Jones, "Entrusted with a Treasure," *The Discipleship Project*, Elementary Level (Hazelwood, MO: Pentecostal Publishing House, Fall 2015) 39.

CHAPTER 6 GRASSHOPPERS WITH SKIN

1. Dottie Rambo, "The Holy Hills of Heaven Call Me," John T. Benson Publishing Company, 1968.

2. This chapter relies on James D. G. Dunn's *The Theology of Paul the Apostle* (Grand Rapids, MI: Eerdmans, 2006) 51–78.

CHAPTER 8 A GRASSHOPPER BY ANY OTHER NAME

1. Lewis and Demarest, *Integrative Theology,* 127, 139.

2. Rachel Thorn and David Molina, "You Are Valuable," *Beautiful Things* (Hazelwood, MO: Link247 Curriculum) available at www.link247.org.

3. Glenn Murphy, *The Called Man: Properly Discerning the Call of God on Your Life* (Bloomington, IN: WestBow Press, 2013) 37.

4. Carol Clemans, "Self-Mutilation–Why?" *IBC Perspectives* (25:6) 16.

5. Paul Brand and Philip Yancey, *Fearfully and Wonderfully Made: A Surgeon Looks at the Human and Spiritual Body* (Grand Rapids, MI: Zondervan, 1980) 47.

CHAPTER 9 HOLY GRASSHOPPERS

1. David K. Bernard, "Holiness" in *Apostolic Study Bible* (Hazelwood, MO: Word Aflame Press, 2014) 191.

2. Ibid., page 191.

3. Dr. James Littles Jr. has greatly influenced the way I think about holiness. I recommend the Mission of the Church and Introduction to Pastoral Care courses offered at Urshan Graduate School of Theology (http://www.ugst.edu).

4. Homer U. Ashby, Jr. *Our Home Is over Jordan: A Black Pastoral Theology* (St. Louis, MO: Chalice Press, 2003).

5. Andrea Thompson, "And the Rainiest City in the U.S. Is . . ." NBC News, http://www. nbcnews.com/id/18827213/ns/technology_and_science-science/t/rainiest-city-us/#. VxwCUzArLic. May 23, 2007.

6. J. Mark Jordan, *A Short Book about You* (Sylvania, OH: JRJ Inspirations LLC, 2009) 33.

CHAPTER 10 GRASSHOPPERS IN NEED OF GRACE

1. Eric S. Blake and Ethan J. Gibney, "The Deadliest, Costliest, and Most Intense United States Tropical Cyclones from 1851 to 2010 (and Other Frequently Requested Hurricane Facts)," The National Hurricane Center, http://www.nhc.noaa.gov/pdf/nws-nhc-6.pdf. Aug 2011.

2. Tim Padgett, "Changing the Hurricane Culture," *Time*. http://content.time.com/time/nation/article/ 0,8599,1102993,00.html. September 8, 2005.

3. Anita Kumar, Alex Leary, Jennifer Liberto, and Chris Tisch, "Towns: 'We got smashed,'" *St. Petersburg Times*. http://www.sptimes.com/2005/09/26/news_pf/Worldandnation/Towns___We_got_smashe.shtml. September 26, 2005.

4. Donald Miller, *Blue Like Jazz: Nonreligious Thoughts on Christian Spirituality* (Nashville, TN: Thomas Nelson, 2003) 85–86.

5. Murphy, *The Called Man*, 42.

CHAPTER 12 GOLIATH-SIZED GRASSHOPPERS

1. Everett L. Worthington Jr., *Humility: The Quiet Virtue* (West Conshohocken, PA: Templeton Press, 2007) 270.

2. N. Graham Standish, *Humble Leadership: Being Radically Open to God's Guidance and Grace* (Lanham, MD: Rowman & Littlefield, 2003) xiii.

3. Everett L. Worthington, Jr., *A Just Forgiveness: Responsible Healing without Excusing Injustice* (Westmont, IL: InterVarsity Press, 2009) 141.

4. Sheila Murray Bethel, *A New Breed of Leader: Eight Leadership Qualities That Matter Most in the Real World: What Works, What Doesn't, and Why* (New York, NY: Penguin, 2009) 336.

5. Richard Bauckham, *Jesus and the God of Israel: God Crucified and Other Studies on the New Testament's Christology of Divine Identity* (Grand Rapids, MI: Wm. B. Eerdmans Publishing Co., 2008) 45.

6. Timothy Keller, "The Advent of Humility" in *Everyday Matters Bible for Women—NLT: Practical Encouragement to Make Every Day Matter* (Peabody, MA: Hendrickson Publishers, 2012) 1440.

7. William Emmanuel Booth Clibborn, "Down from His Glory," composed 1921 (public domain).

CHAPTER 13 GRASSHOPPERS AT WORK

1. Edward G. Harris, *God and Our Daily Work* (Philadelphia: The University of Pennsylvania Press, 1958) 9.

2. Chris Isidore and Tami Luhby, "Turns out Americans Work Really Hard . . . But Some Want to Work Harder," CNN Money, http://money.cnn.com/2015/07/09/news/economy/americans-work-bush/. July 9, 2015.

3. Darrell Cosden, *The Heavenly Good of Earthly Work* (Peabody, MA: Hendrickson Publishers, Inc., 2006) 4.

4. Gary Erickson, *How Bivocational Pastors Understand the Theology of Work*, Dissertation, Covenant Theological Seminary, http://covenantlibrary.org/etd/2014/Erickson_Gary_DMin_2014.pdf, 132.

5. Ibid., page 3.

6. Ibid., page 5.

7. Ibid., page 7.

8. R. Paul Stevens, *The Other Six Days: Vocation, Work, and Ministry in Biblical Perspective* (Vancouver, BC: Regent College Publishing, 1999) 72.

9. Idleman, *Gods at War,* 186.

10. Brand and Yancey, *Fearfully and Wonderfully Made*, 178.

11. Lester DeKoster, *Work: The Meaning of Your Life* (Grand Rapids: Christian's Library Press, Inc., 1982) 1–2.

CHAPTER 14 GRASSHOPPERS WERE BORN TO DREAM

1. "In God's Image," Word Aflame Curriculum (Hazelwood, MO: Pentecostal Publishing House, Fall 2010, Lesson 3) 21.

2. Lewis and Demarest, *Integrative Theology*, 153, 157.

3. Dale Carnegie, *A Combined Edition of How to Win Friends and Influence People and How to Stop Worrying and Start Living* (Hauppage, NY: Dale Carnegie & Associates, 1984) 260.

CHAPTER 15 GRASSHOPPERS WITH EARS

1. Should you be sucked into the world of insect trivia, see Jayne Yack and Ron Hoy's "Hearing" in Vincent H. Resh, Ring T. Cardé's *Encyclopedia of Insects* (Burlington, MA: Academic Press, 2003) 498–505.

2. David S. Norris, *I Am: A Oneness Pentecostal Theology* (Hazelwood, MO: Word Aflame Press Academic, 2009) 18.

3. For this section I have relied on the helpful survey of the historical development of anthropology in Lewis and Demarest's *Integrative Theology*.

4. Hall and Bernard, *Doctrines of the Bible*, 117.

5. David Nelson, "Voicing God's Praise: The Use of Music in Worship," *Authentic Worship* (Eds. Herbert Bateman IV. Grand Rapids, MI: Kregel, 2002) 149.

6. Lewis and Demarest, *Integrative Theology*, 132.

7. Ibid., page 151.

8. Ibid., page 152.

9. Brand and Yancey, *Fearfully and Wonderfully Made*, 40.

10. Yes, we have changed the name of this person. However, she also gave us permission to use her story. I can report that God has ministered to Clarissa in profound ways, and today she serves in ministry, for which we give God glory.

CHAPTER 16 ONE GRASSHOPPER AMONG MANY

1. "National Hug Your Cat Day," Punchbowl http://www.punchbowl.com/holidays/national-hug-your-cat-day.

2. Sharon K. Farber, "Why We All Need to Touch and Be Touched," *Psychology Today* https://www.psychologytoday.com/blog/the-mind-body-connection/201309/why-we-all-need-touch-and-be-touched. September 11, 2013.

3. Brand and Yancey, *Fearfully and Wonderfully Made*, 138.

4. For more, see Robert D. Putnam, *Bowling Alone: The Collapse and Revival of American Community* (New York: Simon and Schuster, 2000).

5. For more, see Randy Frazee's *The Connecting Church 2.0* (Grand Rapids, MI: Zondervan, 2013).

6. My understanding of these concepts has been shaped by the scholarship of James Littles and particularly his course "Mission of the Church" at Urshan Graduate School of Theology.

7. Lewis and Demarest, *Integrative Theology*, 129.

8. Brand and Yancey, *Fearfully and Wonderfully Made*, 148–49.

CHAPTER 17 GRASSHOPPERS UNDER A MAGNIFYING GLASS

1. See Wayne Cordeiro's *Leading on Empty: Refilling Your Tank and Renewing Your Passion* (Minneapolis, MN: Bethany House Publishers, 2010).

2. Rachel Thorn and David Molina, "You Are Valuable," *Beautiful Things* (Hazelwood, MO.: Link247 Curriculum) available at www.link247.org.

3. David K. Li, "Single Adults Now Outnumber Married Adults," *The New York Post*. http://nypost.com/2014/09/09/single-adults-now-outnumber-married-adults/. September 9, 2014.

4. Jaron Lanier, *You Are Not a Gadget: A Manifesto* (New York: Knopf, 2010) 39.

5. Frederick M. Lehman, "The Royal Telephone," composed 1919 (public domain).

6. Joe Robinson, "Is Social Networking Destroying Our Social Lives?" *The Huffington Post*. http://www.huffingtonpost.com/joe-robinson/social-network_b_816d.html. November 17, 2011.

7. Stephen Marche, "Is Facebook Making Us Lonely?" *The Atlantic*. http://www.theatlantic.com/magazine/archive/2012/05/is-facebook-making-us-lonely/308930/. May 2012.

CHAPTER 18 WHEN GRASSHOPPERS ATTACK

1. Lewis and Demarest, *Integrative Theology*, 174.

2. Kenneth Gergen, *The Saturated Self: Dilemmas of Identity in Contemporary Life* (New York: Basic Books, 1991) 15–16.

3. Mildred Alexander, "The Development of the Self-Concept," Report of the Proceedings of the Forty-Sixth Meeting of the Convention of American Instructors of the Deaf (Indianapolis, IN: Indiana School for the Deaf, 1973) available at http://archive.org/stream/reportofproceedi00fern/reportofproceedi00fern_djvu.txt.

4. Brand and Yancey, *Fearfully and Wonderfully Made*, 48.

5. Lewis and Demarest, *Integrative Theology*, 178.

CHAPTER 19 GRASSHOPPERS ENCOURAGING OTHER GRASSHOPPERS

1. Alexander, "The Development of the Self-Concept."

2. See James E. Hightower Jr.'s *Caring for People from Birth to Death* (New York, NY: Haworth Press, 1999).

3. Jonathan McClintock, "The Approachable and Collaborative Pastor," *The Art of Pastoring* (Eds. Robin Johnston and Lee Ann Alexander. Hazelwood, MO: Word Aflame Press, 2015) 126–27.

4. Lewis and Demarest, *Integrative Theology*, 172.

5. Jordan, *A Short Book about You*, 47.

6. Brand and Yancey, *Fearfully and Wonderfully Made*, 204.

CHAPTER 20 GRASSHOPPERS UNDER FIRE

1. Thomas Reynolds, *Vulnerable Communion: A Theology of Disability and Hospitality* (Ada, MI: Brazos Press, 2008) 53.

2. Lewis and Demarest, *Integrative Theology*, 147.

3. David E. Orton, "We Felt Like Grasshoppers: The Little Ones in Biblical Interpretation." *Biblical Interpretation* 11, no. 3–4 (2003): 502. March 20, 2016.

4. Tenney, "The Greatest Challenge of the Twenty-First Century," 20.

AFTERWORD

1. Sophie Brown, "Julia Roberts Shares Stunning Makeup Free Photo on Instagram Claiming 'Perfect Is a Disease of a Nation,'" *The Huffington Post*. http://www.huffingtonpost.co.uk/2015/09/10/julia-roberts-no-makeup_n_8116856.html. October 9, 2015.

2. Brand and Yancey, *Fearfully and Wonderfully Made*, 23.